Carol Sinclair came to live in Britain in 1979 from her native New Zealand, where she had worked in advertising as a copywriter and creative director, and where she wrote a cookery column. She unblushingly admits that she has no qualifications in the medical field, other than as a patient. During her long search for the causes and possible cure of irritable bowel syndrome, she has read many books on the subject of digestion and nutrition, but she believes nothing compensates for an intimate acquaintance with the symptoms. She lives in Bradford-on-Avon, Wiltshire, writes for magazines and is the author of a book on her husband, the painter Ray Harris-Ching.

Dr Alan Stewart qualified as a doctor at Guy's Hospital, London, in 1976 and spent five years specializing in hospital medicine. He became a member of the Royal College of Physicians (MRCP UK) and worked at the Royal London Homoeopathic Hospital, qualifying as an MF Hom. He is a founding member of the British Society for Nutritional Medicine and Medical Advisor to the Women's Nutritional Advisory Service. He is author of *Tired All the Time* (Optima 1993) and co-wrote the bestselling book *Nutritional Medicine*. He has also contributed to other books including *Beat PMT Through Diet, Beat Sugar Cravings, The Vitality Diet, Inside Science, The Migraine Revolution* and the academic book *Post Viral Fatigue Syndrome*. He lectures and writes articles on various aspects of health, contributes to radio programmes and has appeared on many TV magazine programmes. He lives in Lewes, Sussex, with his wife, nutritional advisor Maryon Stewart, and their four children.

THE
IBS Starch-Free
DIET

Over 200 recipes to relieve the pain and symptoms of IBS

Carol Sinclair

WITH

DR ALAN STEWART

VERMILION

LONDON

To my daughter Tanya, for putting up with so many lectures on 'health' and for lugging my suitcase of pills and potions all around Europe on our holiday, in the bad old days before The Sinclair Diet System.

First published in 1995 in the United Kingdom
by Optima as *The Sinclair Diet System*

5 7 9 10 8 6 4

This revised edition published in the United Kingdom in 1997 by Vermilion, an imprint of Ebury Press

Random House UK Ltd
Random House
20 Vauxhall Bridge Road
London SW1V 2SA

Random House Australia (Pty) Ltd
20 Alfred Street, Milsons Point, Sydney
New South Wales 2061, Australia

Random House New Zealand Limited
18 Poland Rd, Glenfield
Auckland 10, New Zealand

Random House, South Africa (Pty) Limited
Endulini, 5a Jubilee Road, Parktown 2193, South Africa

Random House UK Limited Reg. No. 954009

A CIP catalogue record for this book is available from the British Library

ISBN 0 09 181513 4

Typeset in Palladia by Solidus (Bristol) Limited
Printed and bound in Great Britain by Mackays of Chatham plc

Papers used by Vermilion are natural, recyclable products made from wood grown in sustainable forests.

CONTENTS

ACKNOWLEDGEMENTS

I would like to thank the following people: the doctors at Addenbrooke's Hospital, Cambridge, and the producers of a television documentary about their work, who first gave me the idea that I might be able to eliminate IBS symptoms with diet.

Dr Alan Stewart, firstly for being the only doctor to take my symptoms seriously and refer me to St Mark's Hospital in London, and secondly for believing in my starch theory.

My science teacher at Wellington Girls' College, New Zealand, who in 1953, much against my inclination, taught me the basics of food chemistry; which information, lying redundant in my brain for many years, was there to be recycled when I needed it most.

Mr C. Richards, C.Chem., MRSC, of Nestlé UK Ltd., who was so helpful in my search for starch research.

Mr A. Elliot, B.Pharm., MRPharmS, my local chemist, who reminded me of the simple method for testing starch (a piece of information lost in the filing system of my brain until he mentioned it) and which has been so important.

Grace Rockel, my mother, for letting me spend many hours as a child messing up her kitchen and learning how to cook.

Ray Harris-Ching, my husband, for his unwavering support and (although an artist and not in the least interested) for listening patiently over and over again to one theory after another as to the reasons for IBS.

1

For years doctors said the pain in my gut was 'all in the mind' – they were wrong

It was always the same. The doctor would cast a jaded glance in my direction and then frown down at the prescription pad as he scrawled a few lines.

'Hmmm. Spastic colon,' he'd mumble. 'Irritable bowel syndrome – IBS, it's called now. It's due to tension. Emotional problems,' he'd look up wearily – not at me – through me. 'You'll have to learn to relax.' He'd hand me the script. 'Best I can do, I'm afraid – a course of tranquillisers. See how you go with this – oh, unless you'd like some counselling ... a stress management course ...?'

Once again I would be struck dumb with disappointment. I didn't actually blame the doctor. I'd heard it so many times before, that I knew he was repeating the only information available to medical science – but I didn't believe it. Sure, I had problems and stress ... who didn't? But why was it that friends, whose lives were just as stressful, didn't also have IBS? What was the cause of those awful symptoms of pain and bloating after eating? Why, after a modest meal, did I begin to feel as if I'd eaten a huge Christmas dinner, followed by a disquieting ache or small nagging jabs of pain, which, before the night was out, would turn into waves of agony, surging through my distended stomach – often worse than labour pains? If this was IBS, it was more stressful than the stress that was supposed to have caused it!

If you're an IBS sufferer, you'll have been through all this many times. Even to have one's condition diagnosed – given a name – is a relief. That is, until you discover that no one can offer a cure for IBS.

'Think of it as migraine in the gut,' one doctor said to me. 'It's as if you're crying inside...' But I knew I wasn't. I went through the whole gambit of being asked leading questions about my private life ... how did I get on with my husband? Was I under too much tension at work? Sometimes for a change, doctors would make vague references to 'modern living' or 'all those chemical sprays'. But usually it was the stress factor they believed was the cause of the agonising bouts of pain and bloating that mysteriously struck me down again and again. Their explanations were always vague, but determined: it was as a result of early childhood experiences – an unhappy marriage – psychological factors – all in the mind.

None of it rang true to me, because no matter what they said was the cause, when they began offering their explanations, my memory would flash back to the image of a little girl, no more than four years old, lying on the kitchen floor doubled up with pain, while her mother looked down with baffled exasperation, saying to a friend standing beside her that the doctor had told her that some people had a lower pain threshold!

That was me nearly 50 years ago, before 'modern living' and the use of chemical sprays on food. The 'lower pain threshold' theory always irritated me, even as a child, because I knew it meant I was a wimp. But in other ways I was a happy, well-adjusted child, living a normal family life. So I tried not to make too much fuss about the bouts of pain and bloating. I assumed my no-nonsense mother and the various doctors she'd taken me to were right and I was abnormally sensitive.

There was one contributing factor: I had always been constipated, even as a baby, and my mother assumed, as did everyone else, that the pain was part of the constipation. She was advised to fill me up with what we now call fibre. Fruit, vegetables, brown bread, bran muffins, prunes and dried apricots were always part of my daily diet. It probably helped my constipation, but as I discovered years later, it didn't do anything for the IBS agony. In fact all that bran and wholewheat bread just made it worse.

As I got older, the pain didn't really interfere with my life – it *was* my life. Although I didn't have it every day, at least every couple of weeks I would have a bad bout, usually in the evening after the main meal. It didn't matter so much when I could go to bed and curl up with a hot-water bottle, but when

I started dating, the spectre of the pain and bloating would begin to haunt me. The evening would end with me gritting my teeth in agony and going home early when I should have been dancing the night away.

For years during which I had a successful career, married and became a mother, I plodded on, some days in pain, some days all right, but no days, I now realise, feeling really well. But if you've never experienced feeling really well, you don't know what you're missing

In my early-thirties after a number of unhappy years, my marriage ended in divorce and life began to get very much better. My career in advertising was blooming. I began to feel more confident and financially secure than I had for a long time. But despite this new era of happiness, I was experiencing more and more frequent bouts of IBS pain. Finally a friend became concerned when, during a dinner party, I was so obviously in pain that he had to take me home. He persuaded me to consult a specialist and after a series of barium X-rays, I was told I had a congenitally deformed bowel and that I must stay 'regular'. This advice seemed easy enough to follow. I started taking laxatives. A few at first, then more and more. I started on Dulcolax and Picolax, but was then prescribed products such as Normacol (which I loathed) and finally switched to Sennacot under the impression that it was a safer, herbal remedy.

A few years later I remarried and, with my daughter, came to live in Britain. At a time when I was happier than ever before, I began having more pain, more frequently than ever before. In an effort to keep 'regular', this being the only advice I had ever been given, I was now taking 35 Sennacot a night – and every morning I felt dreadful. To this, I added various herbal remedies, all of which promised to aid digestion. My daily intake of greenish, strange-smelling pills was enormous! My daughter remembers a trip we took to the Continent together when I had to take a separate small suitcase for my pills and potions. She's never forgotten the nuisance of dragging this bag, embarrassingly clanking with pill bottles, all over Europe.

I consulted more doctors and tried everything and anything that might help. I drank copious pints of water every day, consumed litres of live yoghurt, pounds of slippery elm, evening primrose oil, lecithin, vitamin supplements and any other remedy that promised the magic goal of better health. I tried relaxation exercises, massage, Zen, meditation, homeopathy – but nothing worked for me. My private life had never been happier, but no one would have believed it – I was taking on all the hallmarks of a miserable neurotic.

And then my luck changed. One night I happened to see a documentary on television about Addenbrooke's Hospital in Cambridge, where doctors were beginning to believe that irritable bowel syndrome, among other chronic conditions, was caused by food intolerance. As I listened to the symptoms described, I realised it was *my* pain and bloating they were talking about – and they said they believed that eliminating wheat flour from the diet could eliminate the symptoms.

The next day I gave up everything I could think of that contained wheat flour. I didn't eat a single piece of bread or cake or pastry or pasta and that evening, for the first time for weeks, I had a pain-free night. Of course, it might have been simply coincidence, I thought. There was only one way to find out – I would keep on eliminating wheat flour. I hated the idea of giving up all the foods I loved most, and I comforted myself with the belief that it probably wouldn't work for long and then I could start eating them all again.

But it did work. Within two to three days I was feeling dramatically better. I decided to stay on the diet. It wasn't easy. As well as no bread, cakes, pastry and pasta, I had to give up battered fish, gravy, sauces, trifle, steamed puddings, crumble-topped puddings, sausages (they contain breadcrumbs) and a host of other foods I'd always loved. I also found that all cooked beans and lentils brought on IBS – but at least, I thought, I could still eat potatoes and rice.

About this time I experimented with oatmeal, rye bread and gluten-free baking mixes made for coeliacs (people who suffer from Coeliac Disease, a condition which prevents them from digesting the protein in gluten and/or wheat and rye) hoping I would be able to eat these, but it made no difference. My IBS was just as bad – and the bread made from the baking mixes tasted awful so I gave up eating all grain-based foods and all lentils.

For about a year, all went well. Then the symptoms came back. I was shocked and miserable. The diet had worked so well for such a long time – what had gone wrong? I couldn't accept that it was anything other than the food I was eating. It obviously wasn't only food made from grain – after all, beans and lentils were amongst the worst culprits. What was it that these foods had in common? I decided it could only be starch. I knew potatoes and rice also contain starch, so I gave them up too and the pain and bloating went away again.

For quite a while all went well – and then the symptoms came back. Nevertheless, I couldn't believe it was my starch theory that was at fault, so I didn't give up. I now knew what it was like to be free of pain and bloating and I wanted to feel like that again. After a lot of thought I realised that every time I ate cooked vegetables, the symptoms returned. Raw vegetables and cooked or raw fruits caused no problems. But why?

I tested my theory, and every time I ate cooked vegetables, green or root, the symptoms returned. Then I remembered a very crotchety chemistry teacher – about a thousand years ago, it seemed – teaching us that vegetables contain starch and drawing diagrams on the board, showing how the cell walls of vegetables are changed during cooking, releasing the starch. If my scratchy memory was to be trusted, once again my starch theory was being proved right, and that teacher deserved a medal! Fruits contain a sugar called fructose, that's why I could eat them either raw or cooked.

Eureka! I thought I had cracked it. I gave up all starch, forever. My diet consisted of meat, cheese, eggs, salads, fruit, ice cream, yoghurt, cream, milk and starch-free sweets such as chocolate, as well as coffee, tea and alcohol – and I felt great.

Then the symptoms came back! I was devastated. I searched every item of my diet for possible hidden sources of starch and it occurred to me that perhaps some tablets I had been prescribed might contain starch to bind them. I asked my doctor, who looked at me as if I was mad and said he couldn't help me. I then asked the local chemist, who looked up his book and said only the active ingredients in pills and tablets had to be listed. Anything else, such as starch or gelatine which might hold the pill together, was not included in his book.

So, I phoned the drug companies. It took a lot of fast talking to convince them I was not a reporter trying to dig up dirt on them, but in the end they confirmed my suspicions. Most pills and tablets contain rice or maize flour. Even these tiny amounts of starch were causing my symptoms. Luckily my doctor could prescribe liquid versions of the medications I needed to take, so the symptoms disappeared again.

When I was really sure it was starch that was causing my problems, a lot of things fell into place. I remembered how well I'd felt years ago when I'd gone on various 'Lose-10-pounds-in-two-weeks' diets, consisting of nothing but salad, steak and grapefruit. The feeling of well-being that I'd always associated with losing weight had in reality been the elimination of starch from my diet.

I also remembered how, when my marriage had dramatically fallen apart and I'd eaten hardly anything for a couple of weeks, despite terrible unhappiness, I'd had no IBS symptoms. In fact, on thinking back, the times I'd suffered emotional trauma and lost my appetite were the times I was free from IBS symptoms. I could actually remember thinking, on one occasion, that at least I hadn't had to suffer IBS as well as the agony of a breaking heart. How then, did this fit into the 'IBS is caused by stress' theory that doctors had been dishing out for years?

IBS is a complex problem. Over five million people in this country have been diagnosed as suffering from the symptoms. There may be a number of causes, but it's all too easy to convince sufferers that it's all in the mind. Almost everyone experiences stress or emotional problems of some kind, so it's very convenient for doctors to be able to diagnose 'stress' as the cause of a patient's symptoms – no one can argue with it. It's also guaranteed to make many patients feel guilty about their inability to manage their relationships/job/children – all the areas of life we're supposed to be able to cope with. Some of us slink away, vowing to try harder and not bother the doctor again; others opt for the tranquillisers or the counselling course.

I've been told I had an 'IBS personality'. Of course I did! I was often depressed, anxious, neurotic, hostile, miserable and fatigued. Anyone suffering constant, mysterious, undiagnosed pain goes through these moods. Sometimes I used to think perhaps I was a hypochondriac, neurotically producing symptoms of all sorts of illnesses, even convinced I had undiagnosed gall bladder and bowel cancer. I can remember going to bed and crying with weakness and pain, feeling black moods of despair and anger.

That's all behind me now, but it's been a long, long trail. For over 10 years I've been a walking laboratory, testing and retesting food in my own stomach. I've combed the shelves of technical book shops and medical libraries and read so much about the complexities of human digestion and nutrition (most of which I couldn't understand without constant reference to medical dictionaries) that I now have some sympathy for the dilemma of GPs faced with patients with my symptoms. As all the books say, not enough is known about this problem.

I can also see why it has been so difficult to isolate starch as a cause of IBS. Small amounts of starch are unexpectedly present in many foods that are not considered starchy. It is hardly surprising that IBS sufferers who have tried eliminating wheat and gluten foods, and still have the symptoms, have come to the conclusion that diet is not the answer. If you are unknowingly eating starch, you naturally conclude your IBS symptoms are being caused by something else.

Although IBS is always considered a side-effect of either constipation or diarrhoea, I've discovered that it can be separately controlled. A few years ago while I was undergoing a series of X-rays to confirm my mega-colon problem, I was not allowed to take Epsom salts or any other laxatives for 10 days. During that time I stuck to my starch-free diet and although I was constipated the whole time, I had no IBS pain or even bloating.

There are many unanswered questions. Research is beginning to escalate, but in my opinion, much too much emphasis is still being given to the so-called psychological reasons for IBS. I hate to think what would have happened to me had I settled for psychotherapy or counselling or hypnotherapy. I suspect I would now be a complete invalid, without control over my own life.

I still don't know for sure why it is that when I first began the diet, the symptoms were eliminated in stages, beginning with wheat flour and lentils, as I've described. I've learned a lot about starch since I began devising the IBS starch-free diet, what I now call the *Sinclair Diet System*. Wheat flour and lentils are in the polysaccharide group – the most complex of the starches – and therefore, I believe, the most vicious offenders to anyone with a starch intolerance. I can only speculate that as I began to feel free of pain, I became increasingly able to detect milder irritants. More on this in later chapters.

I hope that one day medical science will have the answers to my questions – and best of all, a cure. In the meantime, I eat a virtually starch-free diet and as long as I stick to it I'm free of pain. But I still make occasional blunders. Every now and then a food I didn't realise contained starch causes problems. But now I can control the symptoms. If I make a mistake and have one or two days of pain and bloating, at least I know it will pass. When I'm unsure about any particular food, I just don't eat it. But I've also learned how to test for starch before eating unknown foods – it's a simple and reliable method and chapter 7 tells you how.

On the whole, I am now almost completely free of the awful symptoms of pain and bloating, and life is wonderful. I still suffer from constipation but instead of all those laxatives, I take Epsom salts every night. This old-fashioned remedy was recommended to me by a specialist at St Mark's Hospital in London and I have found it very successful. It's not habit-forming and unlike most other laxatives, it doesn't make you feel ill.

There's no known cure for IBS, so I'm resigned to the fact that I may have to stay on the Sinclair Diet System forever. If I'd known at the beginning how many foods contain starch, and tried to eliminate them all at once, I would have got into a dreadful muddle. I've devised the Sinclair Diet System to show you how to eliminate foods slowly, as and when the IBS symptoms recur, and to test for hidden sources of starch in your food.

The great advantage of trying the IBS starch-free diet is that if starch intolerance is causing your IBS, you'll notice a reduction in your symptoms within a few days. And it's perfectly safe – certainly safer than experimenting with a new course of drugs or psychotherapy. You can also stop the diet at any time and go back to your original way of eating. But if starch is your problem, you won't want to.

To people who have no idea of the suffering of IBS, the idea of eliminating so many of the foods we love best is a terrible option. I always tell them the only thing I'm eliminating is pain! It *is* possible to eat a varied and exciting diet without starchy foods – the recipes are all in this book.

People suffer from IBS in varying degrees. If you notice only occasional pain and bloating, you may like to use some of the recipes on days when you particulary want to avoid the symptoms. All the recipes are thoroughly nutritious and you'll find recipes delicious enough to serve for a romantic dinner or an important party, when you want to feel at your best. If you suffer only mild IBS symptoms, you don't have to switch over completely to the IBS starch-free diet – just use the recipes as and when you wish.

These past few years have been an extraordinary revelation to me of how ill I used to feel. Side-effects of starch intolerance, such as joint pains which plagued me even as a child, have disappeared. I used to feel tired and drained much of the time – now I have masses of energy. And best of all, the lack of IBS pain is so blissful that I'm continually grateful for my lucky break that night when I happened to see the TV documentary that started me off on the trail that led to the starch-free diet – and proved that the pain in my gut *was* in my gut, not in my mind.

2

What is irritable bowel syndrome?

by Dr Alan Stewart

Irritable bowel syndrome or IBS is a common condition in both Western and Oriental populations. We know how common it is because surveys have been conducted asking large groups of both patients as well as the 'normal population' about their bowel habits and whether they have the symptoms that make up IBS. What these surveys reveal is that there is an enormous variation in people's bowel habits and symptoms and that many of the normal population – between 10 and 22 per cent – have some or all of the symptoms of IBS!

Firstly, let us look at the symptoms of IBS and how doctors actually diagnose this condition.

The symptoms of irritable bowel syndrome

The symptoms of IBS all relate to a disturbance in the function of the bowels and include in approximate descending order of frequency:

- Abdominal bloating caused by, as you would imagine, a build up of gas in the bowel.
- Abdominal discomfort or pain caused by spasm of the muscles in the wall of the bowel.
- Constipation (opening the bowels infrequently or hard stools), diarrhoea (loose rather than just frequent stools) or a combination of diarrhoea and constipation.
- Excessive wind, up or down.
- Mucus or slime in the stool.
- Nausea and loss of appetite.

Of course these are fairly common symptoms anyway, many of which we have all experienced from time to time. It is how severe they are and their combination that leads to a diagnosis of IBS.

A group of bowel experts who met in Rome in 1992 described the main symptoms of IBS and how they can be used to make the diagnosis of IBS. The 'Rome criteria' are:

1. At least three months' continuous or recurrent symptoms of abdominal pain or discomfort which is:

- relieved by defaecation;
- and/or associated with a change in frequency of stool;
- and/or associated with a change in consistency of stool.

2. *Plus* two or more of the following, at least a quarter of occasions (i.e. 25 per cent of the time) or days

- more than three stools per day or less than three per week;
- altered stool form (lumpy/hard or loose/watery);
- altered stool passage (straining, urgency or feeling of incomplete evacuation);
- passage of mucus;
- bloating or feeling of abdominal distension.

I will be explaining this in a little more detail in just a moment but as you can see it is the presence of several symptoms and the absence of others that makes doctors think of IBS.

Over the next few pages or so I need to mention some other conditions and symptoms which though similar to IBS are different and require a very different approach to that of IBS. It is therefore important that any doctor asks carefully about a number of symptoms and has the time to examine patients before deciding that the most likely diagnosis is IBS. The sort of symptoms that most doctors will ask for include:

- Is the abdominal pain very severe?
- Has there been a loss of weight?
- Is there any pain or difficulty swallowing food?
- Is there blood in the stools or are they very dark in colour?
- Is there a fever?

Also he or she will need to know:

- Has there been any abdominal operation including appendicectomy (removing the appendix)?
- Is there a near-degree relative (mother, father, sister or brother) who developed cancer of the bowel under the age of 50 years?
- For women, is there any vaginal discharge, period problems or pain on intercourse?

The presence of any one of these points raises the possibility of some condition other than IBS. It is, of course, always advisable to check with your doctor first before embarking upon any change in your diet especially if any of the circumstances above seem appropriate to your situation. Your doctor may need to examine you, arrange some tests or ask you to see a hospital specialist.

Some other problem with the bowel such as colitis – inflammation of the lining of the colon – or diverticulosis – a condition where there are small pouches or diverticulae which develop from the wall of the colon because of weaknesses in its wall — may be diagnosed. The abdominal bloating and discomfort that these two conditions can cause can be influenced by diet and some dietary changes along the lines given in this book may be appropriate, but do check this with your doctor first.

How common is irritable bowel syndrome?

With so many symptoms and different combinations of symptoms to choose from it is perhaps easy to see why IBS is so frequently diagnosed by doctors.

One of the most recent surveys was by a group of specialists from Bristol Royal Infirmary. Doctor Kenneth Heaton and colleagues surveyed nearly 2,000 men and women using a standard questionnaire to find out who had IBS and who went to their doctor with it. The questionnaire asked about many of the symptoms of IBS, including the presence of recurrent abdominal pain, abdominal bloating, a feeling of not having emptied the bowels properly, urgency to open the bowels, watery stools, slime in the stools and the association of pain with any of these symptoms. The presence of three or more of these and some other bowel symptoms was taken as a positive diagnosis of IBS.

A diagnosis of IBS could be made in a total of 13 per cent of women aged between 25 and 69 years and in 5 per cent of men aged between 40 and 69 years. Abdominal pain was the commonest symptom in both men and women, was much more common in women than men and was the main factor that determined whether sufferers of either sex consulted with their doctors or not. It was obvious, however, that many sufferers simply put up with their symptoms. Among the other symptoms, bloating and constipation were two of the commonest and were more likely to occur in women as they got older.

Another large and recent survey from the United Kingdom was conducted by Professor Roger Jones and Susan Lydeard in their survey of some 2,000 adults all of whom lived in the Southampton area. A total of 21.6 per cent (24.3 per cent of women and 18.7 per cent of men) reported symptoms that could be attributed to IBS. Because of some uncertainty about the accuracy of some of the answers it is possible that these figures over-estimate the problem, but the minimum figure from this survey is 15.4 per cent or two out of every 13 adults in the population. Of those who responded to the survey and had IBS symptoms, only one third had been to see their doctor and less than half of these had been referred on to a hospital specialist.

The commonest age group for women to experience IBS symptoms was 30 to 49 years and surprisingly for men it was 20 to 39 years. Diarrhoea was reported as a more common problem than constipation in men.

IBS was not more common among smokers and the chance of developing it did not seem influenced by social class. Also a greater proportion of those with IBS symptoms made use of strong pain-killing drugs of the sort prescribed by doctors for arthritis and used in the treatment of painful periods. These drugs are known to irritate the bowel and can cause diarrhoea.

Why do some people develop irritable bowel syndrome?

It is quite clear that the vast majority of those who are unfortunate enough to develop IBS have not always had trouble with their bowels. For many there was an often slow and subtle change in the way that their bowels worked and in particular reacted to stress and the foods that they ate. What could have led to this change?

The kind of factors or health problems that at times lie behind or seem to trigger IBS include:

- Gynaecological problems – such as fibroids or heavy periods.
- Bowel infections – such as gastroenteritis or after a parasitic infection.
- Operations – especially if it involves the bowel.
- Radiotherapy treatment for cancer.
- Drugs – particularly after antibiotics.
- Dietary change – possibly caused by eating foods that are hard to digest.
- Digestive problems.

The symptoms of IBS can improve if the associated health problem is tackled. Anyone for whom one or more of these factors would seem to be relevant should, of course, be consulting with their doctor about it if they have not already done so.

The last category of digestive problems is the one that is most difficult to assess. The first point to make is that those with irritable bowel syndrome do not have a major disturbance in their ability to digest food. Serious disturbance in digestion usually results in weight loss of more than a few pounds or nutritional deficiencies resulting in anaemia, a pale complexion, severe tiredness and loss of appetite.

But it is quite possible that there is a more subtle disturbance in digestion, not severe enough to cause weight loss, but bad enough to affect the way the bowel, especially the last part of it, works. This could be the case in those who have difficulty with certain starch-rich foods. For example, there are some rare conditions where there is a genuine difficulty in the digestion of certain dietary sugars and these always cause abdominal symptoms of bloating, discomfort or pain and diarrhoea or an erratic bowel pattern. These dietary sugars that escape digestion pass into the large bowel or colon where they are rapidly broken down by the resident bacteria there to produce gases and acids that irritate the bowel.

A mild version of this sequence of events could occur in those with IBS who are unable to tolerate certain starch-rich foods. Indeed this is known to occur in all of us with a type of starch present to a small but variable degree in many foods called 'resistant starch'. It appears that we really know little about how much people vary in their ability to digest different starches and only very recently have scientists begun to tell us just how much 'resistant starch' is in some foods and what aspects of food preparation influence the digestibility of starch.

Fortunately there is enough information to help you sort out the wood from the trees or the indigestible from the digestible. There is much more on this in the next few chapters, but first a few words about stress as this is the other main factor that is known to influence IBS.

Stress

There is very good evidence that when many of us are under one kind of stress or another there is a change in the way our guts function. This usually means an increase in the contractions of the muscles of the gut, which can lead to a substantial increase in pressure inside the gut and consequently to pain. Experiments have shown that the type of stress that can do this is driving in London rush-hour traffic or listening to loud music.

Most of us have experienced exam nerves and the effect that this can have on how our bowels work. Even going away on holiday and a break from our routine can cause a change in how our bowels work. Also, in women, the rate at which food moves through the bowel is influenced by the menstrual cycle. The rate slows down in the week or few days before the onset of menstruation and the arrival of the period can be marked by a need to nip off to the toilet to open the bowels with the passage of a rather loose stool.

So our bowels are influenced by the amount of stress our body is under and factors such as our hormonal balance. Now, to understand just how our diet can influence us and the symptoms of IBS, I need to explain first of all about how the digestive system works and what are the main components of the normal diet.

3

How normal digestion behaves

by Dr Alan Stewart

Knowing how the gut works is vital to understanding the theory behind the Sinclair Diet System. Though the process of our digestion is enormously complex, dynamic and indeed fascinating, there are some relatively straightforward aspects that I think most readers will grasp fairly easily. I do not wish to blind you with science or mislead you that I am putting forward a concept that I discovered. The vast majority of the information that follows is in most standard scientific and medical works on digestion and nutrition. (See diagram on p. 23.)

Our digestion

The purpose of our digestive system is to break down the foodstuffs that we consume into small and simple forms that can be absorbed and then be used by our bodies for energy production, normal cell function, growth and repair.

There are several clear steps in the process of digestion. After eating (a process known as ingestion) the food is broken down by mechanical and chemical means. Firstly, our teeth help grind up the food into smaller particles that then allow the chemicals and digestive enzymes to finish the task. Chewing is very important in the digestion of certain foods, and it is very necessary when it comes to the digestion of fibre-rich or starch-rich foods. Most of us have a pretty good idea what will happen if we swallow some sweetcorn whole without chewing it. Many of us have allowed the mechanised millstones that process whole-wheat and other grains into white flour and other less nutritious processed foods to replace the function of our teeth. Not surprising then that consumption of the ultimate processed and most easily digested of 'foods', white sugar, leads to the teeth themselves being made redundant.

In the mouth, as well as the grinding effect, the saliva contains an enzyme that helps in the preliminary breakdown of starch. An enzyme is a large and complex chemical that has a very specific function: to make a chemical reaction of some kind take place. This enzyme in saliva is called amylase and works to break down the two types of starch called amylose and amylopectin into their constituent sugars. Starch itself cannot be absorbed and used by the body as it is, but its constituent sugars can. So amylase gets to work by chopping up starch initially into groups of five or six sugars arranged in a line. The original parent starch can contain several tens or even thousands of individual sugars. In the mouth this process can only go on for a few seconds but does continue in the stomach until it is stopped by the high level of acid in its digestive juices.

The stomach isn't a very friendly place. Its unique characteristic is to produce a large amount of hydrochloric acid strong enough to dissolve iron nails and other metals. That isn't its purpose of course. This acid does two things: firstly, it rapidly kills off most uninvited bacteria and other malevolent bugs, though some do get through occasionally, and secondly it helps to break down the structure of most foods that are rich in protein and carbohydrate. Protein-rich foods are digested by a combination of the hydrochloric acid and the enzyme pepsin. This enzyme acts like amylase chopping up long complex molecules of protein into their simple components called amino acids. These can be absorbed later on. Very little is absorbed from the stomach itself. An exception to this is alcohol – remember drinking on an empty stomach and just how quickly it can affect you?

This slurry of acid, partially digested food and fluid leaves the stomach to pass into the duodenum where digestion can begin in earnest. In the duodenum, a set of quite different digestive juices comes into play. From the liver comes a yellow-green fluid called bile. This is made by the cells of the liver on a continuous basis, is collected and concentrated by the gall bladder – a small sac attached to the under-surface of the liver – and is squeezed out of the gall bladder in response to a fatty meal. Bile contains specialised chemicals that help dissolve fats in the same way that washing-up liquid and soaps do.

The fat is then digested by a specific enzyme from the pancreas. This pale gland lies just behind and below the stomach and produces enzymes that help digest fats, protein and carbohydrates. These do not work until the acid from the stomach is neutralised, and the pancreas also produces another chemical, bicarbonate, which does this. The arrival of bile and pancreatic juices thus allows the food to be digested down to small and absorbable units derived from the original fats, protein and carbohydrates that we eat.

The digestive organs have a complex system of gauging the need for these digestive enzymes with each meal. There are several hormones that are released from the stomach and the duodenum that inform the pancreas, gall bladder and adjacent bowel as to how much of these digestive enzymes are needed. The amount of the hormones released depends on the composition of the meal. Interestingly, it appears that the system for starch digestion relies upon one main hormone, whereas several are involved in the digestion of fats and protein.

After the duodenum the digesting mixture of food passes into the jejunum (part of the small intestine) where the majority of absorption takes place. The jejunum has a highly specialised lining that is delicately folded so that a large surface area, equal to that of a tennis court, is concentrated into a few feet of bowel. Absorption of fats, amino acid and sugars can take place rapidly in this part of the bowel. The starch molecules which were originally gigantic have been broken down by the salivary and pancreatic amylases into units mostly containing two sugar molecules. These are called di-saccharides and are further split into two individual sugars by enzymes that reside in the delicate internal surface of the jejunum. Only the single sugars can be absorbed.

Despite the presence of these powerful enzymes the diges-tion of food is not 100 per cent. Firstly, the fibre in food is by definition not digestible because the amylase in saliva and that from the pancreas are not able to break down cellulose and other similar types of fibre. Additionally, though the starch in our diets could be fully digested it is normal for up to 10 per cent to escape digestion. The small amount of starch in our diet that resists digestion does so because the enzymes may not physically have access to the starch, as in some seeds and partly milled grains, or because of changes in the food which occur during cooking. A small amount of protein and fat also escapes the digestive mêlée.

These undigested portions of our diets leave the small bowel to pass into the large bowel or colon. Here digestion has ended and a very different process is taking place. The normal large bowel is inhabited by billions of bacteria: mostly innocuous but some are potentially disease-producing. Their function in the colon is to feed off the undigested or partially digested remains of our food with the important consequence that they will produce a variety of acids and gases. If produced to excess, these can easily contribute to the symptoms of irritable bowel syndrome. In essence any food that has been difficult to digest in the first part of the bowel will be fermented and broken down in the last part of the bowel, the colon. The result in some cases will be abdominal bloating and wind, sometimes with diarrhoea or constipation. This can happen with starch-rich foods quite easily and some people may be particularly prone to this type of food intolerance.

To better understand this we need to know more about the components of a normal diet.

The normal diet

Even if you don't believe that diet has a major influence on health it surely will come as no great surprise to learn that the type of diet you eat is the main factor determining just how your bowel will work. This idea, though simple, has only recently been appreciated and only after a lot of research work by many specialists. Even so, not all doctors agree that diet is that important and there is certainly little agreement as to which diet is the most effective for those with IBS. Rather than take you through all of the studies and arguments for and against, let me summarise the main dietary factors and their influence on the symptoms of IBS.

I would also like to point out that there is considerable

variation from person to person as to what aspect of their diet seems to influence their IBS and that despite very considerable research there are still some significant gaps in our knowledge.

Firstly, a brief outline of the different components of the diet. You now see on most packeted foods a description of its contents and the quantities of protein, fat and carbohydrate that it contains. What do these terms mean?

Protein

Proteins are large complex chemicals rich in the mineral nitrogen and essential for growth and tissue repair. Good sources include all meats, fish, nuts, beans, milk, cheese and eggs and these nutritious foods are also good sources of vitamins and minerals. When someone is truly allergic to a food then their body reacts to one or more of the proteins that makes up that food, as in allergy to cows' milk protein. When severe even a tiny amount of a food containing this type of protein can cause a reaction.

Fat

Fats can be either liquid such as vegetable oils or solid such as butter or the fat in meat. They are exceptionally rich in calories. High intakes of fat can be hard to digest but this is rarely the problem in IBS.

Carbohydrate

Carbohydrates include the simple sugars and the very complex starches of which much more elsewhere. Carbohydrates are, like fat, mainly used as a source of energy. Carbohydrate-rich foods include fruits, vegetables, cereals such as wheat and oats, and lesser amounts are found in almost all other foods except pure oils.

Fibre

Fibre is the term used to describe the carbohydrate-rich components of our diets, which unlike starch escape digestion and pass into the last part of the digestive tract, the large bowel.

Here they are broken down by the billions of healthy resident bacteria. A certain amount of gas, some mild acids and other chemicals are produced which then can be processed by the body but much remains and passes out as waste material. The more fibre-rich foods that we eat the larger the amount of waste material that we pass and, as a rule, the faster it passes from one end to the other.

Vitamins and minerals

Vitamins and minerals are just as essential as protein and calories, except these are needed only in small quantities. Vitamins and minerals are all needed to help certain chemical reactions take place in the body or in the growth or development of certain parts of the body. For example, the mineral calcium is needed to build the structure of bones and teeth, iron is needed for healthy blood and vitamin B is necessary for much of the nervous system. To be nutritious a diet needs to provide a healthy balance of the essential nutrients and not contain too many processed, fatty or sweet foods, as these are all low in essential vitamins and minerals.

Many foods are rich in these essential vitamins and minerals, including all fruit, vegetables, bread especially wholemeal, other wholesome grain products, fortified breakfast cereals, milk, cheese, eggs, meat, fish, beans, peas, nuts and seeds.

Common foods with a poor or negligible content of vitamins and minerals include sugar (white or brown), sweets, cakes, soft drinks, many alcoholic beverages and convenience or fast foods. In this latter category fall certain hamburgers and the like. For example, a McDonald's 'Big Mac' has virtually none of the vitamin B6 that one would expect it to contain from the ingredients listed in its manufacture, and a few years ago a McDonald's apple pie contained no vitamin C and it is consequently now added to the pie and is listed in its ingredients. But when it comes to ensuring a good intake of vitamins and minerals you cannot beat traditional healthy foods.

How the normal diet influences gut function

Now let us look at how different components of the average diet can influence the bowel function.

Dietary component	**Effect on the gut**
Fibre from fruit and vegetables	Speeds up the passage of material through the bowel and increases the bulk and moisture content of the stools.
Fibre from cereals e.g. bran, wholemeal bread and oats	As for fruit and vegetable fibre but can also delay passage of food through the small bowel and in some can lead to more bloating, wind and bowel disturbance.
Fats such as fried foods, dairy products and fatty meats	These take time to digest. They slow the emptying of the stomach and if digestion is poor can lead to diarrhoea.
Protein – animal e.g. meat, fish, poultry, eggs	Usually easy to digest and cause few problems. However, some people can be truly allergic to these (and other) foods.
Protein – vegetarian e.g. beans, nuts and seeds	Can be hard to digest unless cooked thoroughly. May easily cause wind if not or if eaten in large amounts.
Carbohydrates such as potatoes, rice, wheat, oats, barley, rye, corn – maize and others	In theory easily and almost completely digested but not always! The starch that resists digestion can aggravate the symptoms of bloating, discomfort and a disturbed bowel.
Individual foods and beverages Tea	Can slow down the rate at which food moves through the bowel.
Coffee	Often acts as a mild laxative.
Alcohol	Can certainly cause diarrhoea when consumed to excess. Some people may

Peppermint Tea

be intolerant to even small amounts.
Has a relaxing and calming effect on the upper and lower gut.

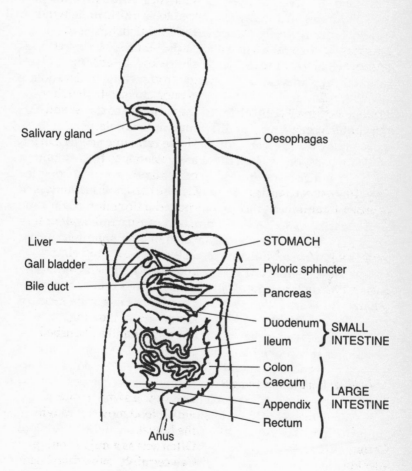

Salivary gland

Oesophagas

Liver

STOMACH

Gall bladder

Pyloric sphincter

Bile duct

Pancreas

Duodenum ⎱ SMALL
Ileum ⎰ INTESTINE

Colon
Caecum
Appendix ⎱ LARGE
Rectum ⎰ INTESTINE

Anus

The digestive system

4

What is starch?

All food is divided into two basic groups: proteins and carbohydrates. Animal products are basically protein; plant products are basically carbohydrate. Some plants also contain proteins and some animal foods also contain carbohydrates. But starch is found mainly in carbohydrates – therefore, foods made from plants cause IBS symptoms for those of us who are starch intolerant.

Plants store carbohydrates in the form of sugars, or saccharides, which are present in different combinations of simplicity or complexity. The very simplest are called monosaccharides which means 'one sugar'; these are *glucose* and *fructose* (found in fruit) and *galactose* (found in milk). The next most complex are called disaccharides or 'two sugars'; these are *sucrose* which is a combination of glucose and fructose (found in sugar cane and sugar beet), *lactose* a combination of galactose and glucose (found in milk) and *maltose*, a combination of two glucose sugars (found in germinating cereals).

The most complex of all are the polysaccharides or 'many sugars', a combination of all the above and others not mentioned. These are called *starch* and are found in a wide range of grains and vegetables and a few fruits.

I have discovered that the more complex the saccharide is, the longer it is cooked and the more I eat, the more trouble it causes! I get more pain and bloating from eating polysaccharides, for example, than from eating disaccharides. Monosaccharides cause me no problems.

It's taken me years to understand which saccharide is which, and which ones cause my IBS. To help me remember, I think of them like this:

Mild-mannered monosaccharides

These are the sweet-tempered, gentle sugars that won't cause you any pain.

- Glucose – found only in grapes.
- Fructose – found in fruit.
- Galactose – found in milk.

Dodgy disaccharides

You have to be careful of these sugars – they're devious and can be dangerous if you eat too many, especially when they're cooked for a long time.

- Sucrose – found in all forms of ordinary sugar, brown and white.
- Lactose – found in milk.
- Maltose – found in germinating cereal seeds.

Painful polysaccharides

These will cause you real trouble. They're the ones that cause the pain and bloating of IBS. Although they're saccharides, they don't look or taste like sugar. Collectively they're known as:

- Starch – found in all grains, lentils and most vegetables, but not in most fruits.

5

What happens when I eat starch and why does it upset me?

by Dr Alan Stewart

This chapter is unavoidably technical but fascinating and essential to understanding the starch-free Sinclair Diet System. Recent developments in the fields of food chemistry and human digestion have caused a substantial change in our view of starchy foods and their effects upon the body.

Essentially there are three main factors that determine how your body will get along with any one type of starchy food. The three main factors are:

- The structure of the starch.
- How it is processed and cooked.
- How it is digested.

We have already considered the process of digestion so let us look at the first two factors in some detail.

The structure of starch

Starch exists in a variety of forms and is widely distributed in many plants. Those plants with a high starch content are regularly used as major food sources. In the plant starch is stored as a fuel supply for the plant itself. It is stored as microscopic granules which are insoluble in water until they are heated or broken down.

When these starch granules are examined further they are found to be composed of collections of starch molecules that are

26

arranged together in different patterns, often being laid down in concentric circles like the rings in a tree trunk. Some of the molecules of starch are grouped together to form crystals similar to granules of sugar. In this way the starch is stored in a very compact form with only a little water present.

When we look closer at the starch crystals an extraordinary pattern appears. Each starch molecule is actually gigantic! It is up to 25 million times larger than the size of a water molecule and can contain up to a million glucose units. It is how these units of glucose are arranged that is so fascinating. There are two types of starch molecules; both are composed of glucose but they each have a very different structure. The simpler of the two is amylose which is essentially a long chain of approximately 1,000 glucose units, with a few small side chains. It usually comprises 15 to 35 per cent of the starch content of most starch-rich foods.

The second type is amylopectin which is much larger and has an overall structure like a tree with a main stem and many side branches which split several times and end not in a leaf but a long chain of 15 to 30 glucose units. The structure is rather like that of a weeping willow. Each of these large tree-like amylopectin structures is then coiled up and packed together with several of its fellows to form a starch granule.

The difference in the texture, appearance and digestibility of many starch-rich foods is explained by the proportions of amylose and amylopectin that are present.

Starch can be further classified, depending upon its digestibility by the human intestine. Some types of starch can be rapidly digested, some are slowly digested and some are never digested and act like fibre as a source of fuel for the bacteria in the large bowel.

Rapidly digestible starch (RDS) is the starch that can be digested to release glucose within 20 minutes of digestion by the enzymes from the pancreas. It is mainly found in foods that have been cooked with heat and plenty of water such as bread or potatoes. The RDS quickly releases glucose and causes a sudden rise in blood glucose levels, virtually as rapid as that caused by consuming glucose itself.

Slowly digestible starch (SDS) is the starch that releases its glucose constituent after 20 minutes and before two hours of digestion by the pancreatic enzymes. Remember that these enzymes only come into play after food has left the stomach and that about two hours later it will be leaving the small bowel and entering the large bowel. So slowly digestible starch will produce a much more gradual rise in blood glucose levels. It is found in wholegrain foods, seeds, pasta and beans. These are the foods that are recommended for diabetics because they are slowly digested and don't cause a sudden rise in blood glucose.

Finally we come to resistant starch, for some the villain of the piece. This in turn comes in three guises. Resistant starch 1 is starch that is physically inaccessible as in that found in whole or partly milled grains, haricot beans or pearl barley. Resistant starch 2 is starch that is just hard to digest. This may vary to some degree from person to person as some people do seem to produce very potent forms of amylase, the main starch-digesting enzyme. Foods such as banana and raw potato are high in this type of starch. As bananas ripen so their content of starch decreases and the content of sugar and resultant sweetness increases. It is easier to digest a fully ripened banana than it is a green one.

Resistant starch 3 is retrograde amylose. Amylose is one of the two main types of starch and is easy to digest when the food containing it is freshly cooked and is eaten while it is still hot. Cooled cooked potato, corn flakes (which are a cooked and cooled food) and, to a lesser extent, bread all contain RS 3 or retrograde amylose.

Thus there is substantial variation in the digestibility of starch. At one extreme it is almost as digestible as sucrose or table sugar and at the other as indigestible as fibre. Now we need to understand a little more about the effect that cooking has on the digestibility of starch.

What happens when starch is processed and cooked?

Starch itself does not dissolve in cold water or even at body temperature of 37° Celsius. Heating a starch-rich food with plenty of water to above 50° Celsius, usually to boiling point of 100° Celsius, is required to break down the starchy food and make it digestible. When a starchy food such as potato is cooked the heating causes the cells of the potato to swell and disrupt. The starch granules inside the cells also swell and the crystals dissolve and the other large starch molecules become semi-dissolved in the water as well. This process of breaking the starch molecule open and partly dissolving it in water greatly increases the ease with which it is broken down by the digestive enzyme amylase. This is why we do not eat raw potato or uncooked rice – they are simply too hard to digest. Also if you do not use enough water when cooking rice then the centre of the rice grain remains hard and 'uncooked'. Some starchy foods such as potato have enough water in them to dissolve the starch they contain so they can be cooked dry as in baking or by microwaving.

Cooking or ageing of a cooked starchy food can greatly increase the amount of resistant starch in the food with the consequence that it is then hard to fully digest and can then, in those who are susceptible, contribute to the symptoms of IBS. For example, when cooked boiled potato is cooled, about 10 per cent of the amylose starch rapidly changes its structure to become resistant starch. This is the cooking process in reverse and it can happen very quickly as food cools. Thus cooled cooked potato can be harder for some people to digest, which is something that you can only discover for yourself by trial and error.

This process of retrogradation also happens more slowly when bread becomes stale. However, bread mainly contains amylopectin and this is more stable with only a small amount becoming resistant starch. In bread this process of retrogradation or staling is partly reversible by reheating the food especially if there is adequate moisture present.

In general freshly cooked foods that are still hot are a lot easier for most people to digest. Starch which escapes human digestion and is known as resistant starch provides a significant source of food for the ever-hungry bacteria in the large bowel. It has only one fate, like fibre the non-starch polysaccharide in our diet, to be turned into gas and mild acids in the large bowel and is a potential cause of the bloating and bowel disturbance for many with IBS.

This effect of cooking and cooling on starch may well explain why some people seem unduly sensitive to the small amounts of 'modified starch' that finds its way into so many modern and convenience foods. Modified starch is any type of starch from wheat, potato, rice or maize that has in some way been processed. This usually means that it has been heated with a varying amount of water for a varying period of time and it will then have acquired certain properties. Modified starch is used to thicken sauces or to give bulk to a food. Unfortunately it will almost always provide a significant amount of resistant starch of mainly type 3 which may well cause digestive problems for some.

How to improve the digestibility of the starch in your diet

Not everyone will have to cut out all starchy foods when following the Sinclair Diet System. There does seem to be a fair degree of variability in our ability to digest starch.

From what is known about the structure and properties of starch and how it is digested, it may be possible to improve your ability to digest starch-rich foods. Here are some tips:

- Chew your food well. This helps to break down the physical barriers to starch digestion, and stimulates the flow of saliva which carries with it the starch-digesting enzyme amylase.
- Eat slowly and don't gulp your food. The longer the food spends actually in your mouth, the more starch is digested. Starch digestion from the amylase in saliva actually continues for a while in the stomach despite the presence of acid.
- Eat cooked food that has not been waiting around for more than a few minutes. The longer it waits and the more it cools the more resistant starch 3 can be formed.
- Do not smoke. This can inhibit the digestive capacity of the pancreas and potentially decrease your ability to digest starch-rich foods.
- Avoid foods and beverages that cause food to move through the intestines too quickly. Coffee is probably the best example of this but any food that irritates your digestive system even if it is low in starch may inadvertently lead to a greater proportion of the starch in your diet being undigested.
- Rest and relax after meals especially a large meal. This will

help your digestion cope with the foods that it has to tackle.

- Have some fat in your diet. Fatty foods delay the emptying of the stomach and generally slow down the rate at which foods move along the digestive tract. So include some dairy products, butter, margarine, and the fat on meat or fish or cooking oils with each meal.

- Perhaps it is also unwise to drink large amounts of fluid with a meal. This might dilute the action of the starch-digesting enzymes or increase the rate of stomach emptying. This is an idea that goes back to the early naturopaths of the 1920s and 1930s.

- Finally some people who are severely intolerant of starch-rich foods may have a more serious digestive problem. Weight loss, diarrhoea or persistent abdominal pain that is anything more than mild would suggest this possibility. The elderly, those with a long history of digestive problems and those who have had an operation on their stomach or intestine need very careful assessment by their doctor or specialist.

It is possible that the problems some people experience with the starch content of foods may lie behind the attraction of some of the advice given in the food combining diets and in the low carbohydrate diets that are recommended by some writers and therapists in the treatment of candida albicans. These two dietary topics have been enormously popular with the public and media alike but have failed to convince the academics. Perhaps there is a scientific basis to the claims made by the protagonists of these dietary therapies and perhaps it relates to starch. The only way to find out is to try it and see.

6

Which foods contain starch?

Starch is the most common and widely eaten food all over the world. It is a major part of a normal diet, contained in all breakfast cereals, breads, cakes, pastries, batters, vegeburgers, rice dishes, pasta – all the most frequently eaten foods. I cannot eat *any* cooked foods containing starch from grains. Even a very small amount causes IBS pain and bloating for me, and perhaps for you too.

Many vegetables release starch when they're cooked but not when they're raw. These can therefore be eaten raw without any IBS problems. A few vegetables do not contain starch, even when they're cooked. These I can eat – but it's not easy to tell the difference just by looking at them. However, there is a simple way of testing to see which vegetables contain starch – I'll tell you how in chapter 7.

I've also discovered that I can eat foods made with sucrose (ordinary table or cooking sugar) in small amounts. For example, I can eat one meringue (made the traditional way without cornflour, of course) but not two. If I eat too much sugar, however, I will experience some bloating and a little pain.

While we're talking about sugars, here's an interesting piece of information about honey. Health foodies have maintained for years that honey is far better for you than sugar (sucrose). But most chemists shake their heads in disbelief, because honey is really only sucrose – a dodgy disaccharide. However, while the honey is being processed through the bee's gut, it is broken down into the mild-mannered monosaccharides, fructose and glucose. Thanks to the hard-working bee, it's pre-digested and must, therefore, be better for those of us with digestive difficulties.

Fruit containing only fructose, can be eaten both cooked and raw, with the exception of bananas – the one fruit that contains starch and cannot be eaten either cooked or raw on the Sinclair Diet System. Rhubarb, which is really a vegetable, also contains starch and can't be eaten.

Meat, fish and eggs do not contain starch and will not cause IBS in starch-intolerant people unless starch is included in the recipe when they are cooked.

Milk, on the other hand, contains the dodgy disaccharide lactose, which causes the symptoms of IBS for some people – a condition known as lactose intolerance. This is most likely to occur in African, Eastern European, Middle and Far Eastern people, or their descendants who for reasons not fully understood, do not secrete the enzyme needed to digest milk, after their mid-teens. In yoghurt or cheese, however, the lactose has already been broken down into a digestible form by bacterial action – which is why yoghurt is a dairy product which is frequently found in Indian recipes.

Some fascinating facts about fructose

I have found that fruit sugar (or fructose) is very much better to eat than ordinary sugar (or sucrose). Fructose is a mild-mannered monosaccharide – a natural sugar found in fruits, honey and vegetables. For most of us fructose can be eaten without causing IBS, however, some may experience bloating and slightly looser stools if they eat too much fruit at one sitting.

Fructose and diabetics

'Fructose is important in the diet of diabetics, since unlike glucose, fructose metabolism is not dependent on insulin.' So says my *Oxford Paperback Reference Concise Medical Dictionary.* The diabetes referred to here is *diabetes mellitus,* or age-onset diabetes, the most common form of the disease.

Diabetes mellitus, as you will know if you have it, is a disorder of the carbohydrate metabolism in which sugars cannot be processed in your body because you do not produce enough of the pancreatic hormone, insulin, which enables the cells to use them to produce energy. The result is that many of the carbohydrates you eat just hang about in your bloodstream in the form of glucose, circulating in abnormally large amounts. This causes *hyperglycaemia*. Your body then tries to use fats as an alternative source of energy. Unfortunately, increased utilisation of fat in this way leads to the accumulation of certain poisonous products of fat metabolism in the liver and bloodstream and this results in convulsions and diabetic coma.

Fructose, however, is the one sugar that does not need to use insulin to be processed into energy in your body. This means that as a diabetic, you can eat sweet foods made with fructose when you cannot eat foods made with sucrose or glucose. Fructose therefore, gives you a safer form of sweetness and additional nutrition. Of course, before you take my word for it, you should discuss this with your doctor. The bibliography at the back of the book will give you the sources of this information, so that he can check the validity.

Fructose is the sweetest of all natural sugars, which means you can use less – giving you fewer calories if you're on a slimming diet. Fructose, therefore, can be used in moderation by diabetics.

Fructose and hangovers

One of the most fascinating facts about fructose is that it increases the rate of alcohol metabolism and can help prevent hangovers! Intravenous administration of fructose has been used successfully in the alleviation of severe alcohol intoxication. Of all the sugars, only fructose has this ability – so remember next time you're planning a party, serve some of the fruit drinks from the recipes in this book and your friends will have only happy memories of your hospitality.

I recommend that you substitute ordinary sugar with either honey or Dietade Fruit Sugar as often as you can. There are other brands of fruit sugar available from health food shops, but Dietade Fruit Sugar is available from most supermarkets. One thing fruit sugar cannot do is to make a crisp meringue or pavlova. You will have to use ordinary sugar for this.

Most processed foods contain a lot of starch

One of the most identifiable characteristics of starch is that it is an excellent binding agent. (I really don't want to bad-mouth starch – it's not its fault I can't eat it – but whenever I'm tempted to feel sorry for myself, I just conjure up an image of a large bucket of pale, gluggy wallpaper paste. Ugh! Anyone can walk away from a bucketful of glue!)

Starch is, in fact, a perfectly wholesome food, and also a very useful one because it is the most efficient way to thicken food and provide the basic 'structure' of much of the food eaten throughout the world. It's the reason why bread and cakes hold their shape and can be light and soft without collapsing. It is used in most medicines to bind them into tablets and pills. It is also often included in manufactured foods which do not normally need to be thickened, such as chutneys or yoghurts, simply to cut down the natural thickening time in the processing. Starch saves money for the producer.

There are many types of starch used in processed food which go under different names. In most countries they are usually identified simply as 'modified starch' or 'modified food starch'. Modified starch can be as commonplace as wheat flour, corn-flour, arrowroot, maize flour, potato flour or rice flour, but some starches are known only to commercial producers. All modified starch, it must be stressed, is perfectly wholesome for normal digestion – but not for those of us who suffer from starch-intolerant IBS.

Here is a list of some you may come across, identified only by E numbers. These are not commonly used yet in the UK but you may find them in processed foods in other parts of Europe.

Modified starch list
*E1400 White or yellow dextrins, roasted starch.
 E1401 Acid-treated starches.
 E1402 Alkaline-treated starches.
 E1403 Bleached starches.
 E1404 Oxidised starches.
 E1410 Mono starch phosphate.
 E1411 Di starch phosphate.
 E1412 Di starch phosphate produced in different ways.
 E1413 Phosphated di starch phosphate.
 E1414 Acetylated di starch phosphate.
 E1420 Starch acetate.
 E1421 Starch acetate produced in different ways.
 E1422 Acetylated di starch adipate.

E1423   Acetylated di starch glycerol.
E1430   Di starch glycerol.
E1440   Hydroxypropyl starch.
E1441   Hydroxypropyl di starch glycerol.
E1442   Hydroxypropyl di starch phosphate.

*Reproduced from *E for Additives* by Maurice Hanssen.

7

How to recognise starch in your food

The most common high-starch foods have a starchy look – they're usually pale and thick! Keep that in mind and you'll find it easy to recognise the foods most likely to cause IBS symptoms. But it's not so easy to recognise starch in other foods.

Often when I thought I had eliminated every possible source of starch from my diet, the dreaded symptoms would return and I would be desperate again. There seemed to be no answer to identifying starch in some food, except to eat it and suffer. And then my friendly local chemist reminded me of the easy test for starch: simply drop iodine onto a sample of the suspect food. (It should not be eaten however.) If it contains starch, the colour of the iodine will darken from orange to shades ranging from inky blue to black. Needless to say, I tested all sorts of food immediately. Flour, bread, cakes, potatoes and rice go a very dark blue-black colour – almost like carbon. Raw sliced vegetables show signs of starch by going greyish around the edges – where the cell wall has been damaged by cutting, I suppose – but it's not enough to cause problems. On meat, cheese, butter, eggs and animal products, the iodine colour remains unchanged (it may tend to go a little darker as it dries). The same is true of most fruits – except bananas, which in varying degrees, depending on how ripe they are, turn dark when tested, proving they're full of starch.

Unfortunately, I sometimes still discover new sources of starch in foods. This is where the iodine starch test is a great help. If the starch content in the food is significant enough to cause IBS problems, it will show up. There are other methods of testing for starch, but the iodine test seems to be very reliable as far as the digestion of starch is concerned, and it's easy and quick.

NB: Test food separately. Do not eat tested food or iodine.

Buy a small bottle of iodine (about 40 to 50 pence) from your local chemist and an eyedropper. Drop a small amount of iodine onto the suspect food, then wait a few minutes to see if the iodine changes from its normal orange colour into shades ranging from reddish-brown to dark inky-blue or even black. Some foods take longer than others to show the starch content. On nutmeg, for instance, it takes about 30 minutes before the iodine drop turns almost black.

It's surprising to discover that some foods which most people believe to be basically protein – such as certain varieties of nuts – contain high quantities of starch. Ground almonds had never caused me problems, so I wasn't surprised when the iodine test showed they contained no starch, but walnuts are a different matter – I discovered that the skin contains starch, while the meat of the nut does not. Cashew nuts are very rich in starch as are chestnuts and sunflower seeds. Peanuts also contain starch. Sadly, some of the foods we think of as 'health foods' have high starch content.

Even some cheeses, such as Brie and Camembert sometimes have starch in their outer white crust, although of course, the main cheese part is protein and fat. This is not always the case and may perhaps be because potato flour or other starch has been used in the final processing. It's always wise to test before eating. If you're unsure about any food, the iodine test will help you to identify quickly and easily whether it's safe for you to eat.

Recently I have made one further discovery: ordinary sugar, i.e. table sugar, castor sugar, brown sugar or raw sugar all of which is processed from cane sugar or sugar beet, can cause problems if I eat too much. This trouble is compounded if the sugar has been cooked too long or at too high a temperature – the scientific term is 'caramelisation'. Caramelisation produces digestive resistant starch or RS.

Sugar can be cooked at low temperatures (as in meringues) or dissolved in cold solutions, as in cold puddings such as ice cream. It's safer eaten in this way, but you can also substitute fruit sugar in almost exactly the same way for most cooking or sweetening. The previous chapter explains why.

Find out what goes into your food

Life becomes much easier when you know a little about cooking. If you've never been much of a cook, now is the time to learn how to identify the ingredients of the food you eat and understand how it is cooked. Unless you know what's in that delicious red wine sauce on the steak, you're taking a risk every time you order it in a restaurant. The steak itself is starch-free, but the sauce could be cooked either with or without starch. If the chef is using traditional French methods of cooking, he will have used butter or cream to *de-glaze* the sauce (just another word for thickening) and you'll be able to eat it. He may, however, be thickening the sauce with cornflour.

If you're not plunged into despair by the idea of trying to get a truthful answer from the waiter, pluck up courage and ask him to find out if the sauce contains flour or cornflour. Explain you are 'allergic' to flour and cornflour (don't begin to confuse him with the word 'starch') and usually you'll find he'll be very helpful. If, however, the waiter doesn't inspire your confidence, it's best to avoid any food you're not sure of – particularly sauces.

Learn to recognise food additives

As we've already shown you in the modified starch list in chapter 6, there may be food additives that contain starch in the food you want to eat. I recommend that you buy a copy of the book *E for Additives: The complete E number guide* by Maurice Hanssen.

Most food additives identified by 'E' numbers appear gruesomely suspicious and get a bad press. However, when you look them up in the 'E' number book, you'll be relieved to find that far from being the dreaded 'man-made chemicals', most are derived from perfectly wholesome plants such as seaweed, or from natural mineral sources which are safe to eat. But sometimes one comes across a food additive that is known to cause digestive problems and this usually means it will cause problems for starch-intolerant people. The 'E' book lists all sources of food additives, which foods they are likely to be added to and all known adverse effects.

8

How to manage the Sinclair Diet System

Plan to try the diet for two weeks. Anyone can go without bread and cakes for two weeks. And instead of feeling miserable at the prospect of giving up these familiar old friends, keep in mind that what you're giving up is pain! If at the end of that time you don't feel any relief from pain and bloating, the Sinclair Diet System is probably not the answer for you, and you can go back to your original diet. But if you experience definite relief from pain, as I did, you'll find it easy to learn what to avoid. Life without the symptoms of IBS is so wonderful I no longer miss the foods that caused it.

- Read the previous chapter carefully, and make sure you have a bottle of iodine and an eyedropper ready to test any food you're unsure about.
- Read the list of ingredients on every can and pack of processed food. (Don't forget to take your reading glasses when you go shopping.) Look out particularly for that little monster 'modified starch'.
- Don't be downhearted if you make mistakes – it's not the end of the world. When your IBS symptoms subside, start again, knowing that now you can overcome the problem.

Start slowly
– eliminate the most common offenders first

Section 1

Grains and cereals   Anything made with, thickened with or mixed with: wheat flour, wholemeal flour, wheatgerm, cracked wheat, matzoh meal, burghul, bulgur, bran, barley, barley flour, pearl barley, semolina, couscous, cornflour, modified

41

starch, cornmeal, maize flour, maize starch, oats, oatmeal, rye, rye flour, polenta, sorghum, tapioca, arrowroot, malt, malt extract, baking powder.

This includes: bread, rolls, buns, croissants, breakfast cereals, muesli, cakes, biscuits, cookies, crackers, pastries, cream puffs, éclairs, pies, flans, quiches, pizzas, battered deep-fried foods, all pasta including canned spaghetti, Italian noodles, egg noodles, wheat noodles, dumplings, doughnuts, pancakes, steamed puddings, batter puddings, bread puddings, crumble-topped puddings, soufflés, custard-powder custards, white sauces, cheese sauce, gravies, sausages, meatloaf, rissoles or any meatballs and mixtures containing breadcrumbs, rusk or modified starch, sandwiches, most pâtés and relishes and chutney. Pills and medication in pill form containing maize starch, modified starch or cornflour.

Lentils and pulses   Anything made with, thickened with or mixed with: soya beans or soy flour, black fermented Chinese beans, haricot beans, Boston beans, kidney beans, lima beans, pinto beans, broad beans, mung beans, dhal, flageolets, gungo beans, pigeon beans, black-eyed beans, aduki beans, black beans, butter beans, Urd beans, chick beans, cannellino beans, borlotto beans, ful medames, rice beans, lablab beans, red, yellow, brown, grey, orange or green lentils, puy lentils, Indian brown lentils, split-peas, chick peas, pigeon peas.

This includes: baked beans, bean salads, soups, casseroles, cassoulets, soy-meat-substitute, TVP, textured vegetable protein in loaves, rissoles or patties, bean sauces, soy bean sauce, tamari sauce, pease pudding, shoyu sauce, fu juk.

Exceptions to the rule: soya bean curd   (Tofu). This is a vegetable protein made from soya milk. According to my testing, it contains very little starch. I have not eaten it myself, but I think it could be eaten on a low starch diet. It therefore would be a good source of protein to vegetarians who are starch intolerant. If you find that it causes IBS symptoms, you will have to eliminate it.

Quorn   is another protein substitute, a myco-protein product made from a plant similar to mushrooms. It is not high in starch but when tested with iodine, it shows the presence of too much starch for me. Some people may be able to eat it.

If symptoms remain or begin to recur
– eliminate the second group

Section 2

Rice products Anything made with, thickened with or mixed with: pudding rice, long-grain rice, brown rice, wild rice, Basmati rice, converted rice, easy-cook rice, American rice, Uncle Ben's rice, Italian rice, Carolina rice, glutinous rice, rice noodles.

This includes: rice pudding, rice salads, fried rice, rice served with Indian, Chinese, Italian or Russian dishes, rice noodles, rice paper, stuffings made with rice, rice cakes, rice crispies, savoury rice snacks, sweet rice snacks.

Potato products Anything made with, thickened with or mixed with: potatoes, potato flour, sweet potatoes, yams.

This includes: potatoes boiled, baked, roasted, scalloped, steamed, fried, battered, deep-fried, candied, chipped; instant potato powder, potato waffles, potato croquettes, crisps, potato salad, potato scones, gnocchi, potato thickening soups, stews and casseroles.

If symptoms remain or begin to recur
– eliminate the third group

Section 3

Cooked fresh vegetables (hot or cold) Anything cooked with, thickened with or mixed with:

- Root vegetables: parsnips, carrots, celeriac, horseradish, beetroot, breadfruit, taro, cassava, white radish, Chinese radish, Daikon radish, navette, salsify, scorzonera.
- Bulbs: leeks, garlic, shallots.
- Pods and seeds: green peas, mangetout, sweetcorn, broad beans, green beans, string beans, runner beans, okra.
- Greens: Savoy cabbage, January king cabbage, frozen broccoli, cauliflower, Brussels sprouts, spring greens, silverbeet, Swiss chard, kale, pak-choi, pe-tsai, kohlrabi.
- Squashes and gourds: pumpkin, butternut, spaghetti squash, custard squash, golden nugget, acorn squash, West

Indian pumpkin, snake squash, marrow.
- 'Vegetable fruits': aubergines, egg plant, red/green/ yellow/orange sweet peppers, chilli peppers, akee, bread-fruit, and avocado. **Note**: avocado, like the banana, is very rich in starch and cannot be eaten at all, either cooked or raw.

These include: any of the above cooked or canned or bottled, hot or cold, which have been boiled, roasted, baked, scalloped, fried, battered, deep-fried, stir-fried, sautéed, creamed, braised, steamed or grilled, in casseroles, stews, soups, pies, flans, quiches, cheese sauces, pastas, pizzas, curries or salads.

Individual reactions seem to be the rule

Some people may have trouble digesting non-starch poly-saccharides, i.e. fibre. These will always be of vegetable origin.

Eat herbs safely but spices with caution

In my experience, most herbs are starch-free, but many spices contain starch. However, *The Composition of Foods* by McCance and Widdowsons, a publication used extensively by food chemistry and food advisory services, gives starch ratings which are sometimes at variance to my tests with iodine.

Here is a list of herbs and spices all rated 'N', according to *The Composition of Foods*, which means that starch is present in significant quantities but there is no reliable information on the amount. Some I have tested myself and can confirm that they show the presence of starch when subjected to the iodine test. But others do not show the presence of starch, no matter how often I test them and regardless of how they are cooked – one of these is garlic powder, which has a very high starch rating (38.5) according to *The Composition of Foods*. I use garlic powder frequently and have never experienced IBS symptoms from it. I can only say with any certainty, use the iodine test and your own judgement. If any foods cause symptoms to recur, eliminate them.

Allspice, anise seeds, asafoetida, caraway seeds, cardamom (ground), cayenne pepper, celery seeds, chilli powder, Chinese five spice, ground cinnamon, coriander (dried and seeds), cumin seeds, curry powder (mixed flavours), *dill (dried and seeds), fennel seeds, fenugreek seeds, Garam Masala, *garlic powder, ginger (fresh and ground), liquorice powder, *mace, *marjoram, *mint, *mustard (powder and seeds), nutmeg (ground), *oregano (fresh and dried), paprika, *parsley (fresh and dried), poppy seeds, *rosemary (fresh and dried), saffron, *sage (fresh and dried), *tarragon (fresh and dried), *thyme (fresh and ground dried), turmeric (ground).

More anomalies and exceptions to the rule

When I first discovered cooked vegetables contained starch, I gave them all up. I've recently, tentatively, begun eating a few varieties, based on information listed in *The Composition of Foods*. The starch ratings of foods listed in this reference range from 0 to 95 (for tapioca). I have discovered that I cannot safely eat anything with a rating over 0.1 (unless, like garlic powder, I have tested it frequently and cannot detect any starch). Foods rated as 0.2, such as fresh cooked mushrooms, sometimes give me some bloating, but no pain. Cocoa powder in cooking causes symptoms, but diluted in a milk drink or in chocolate, it seems fine.

One vegetable I have recently added to my diet is asparagus which, according to the latest supplement to *The Composition of Foods*, contains only a trace of starch when cooked, although canned it contains a more dangerous amount. Much to my delight, I've found asparagus causes no IBS symptoms, so I eat it often.

As I have already mentioned, some of the foods which contain no starch according to these reference sources, do show the presence of starch when given the iodine test; while others, which according to the reference do contain starch, are starch-free when given the iodine test. It has been my experience that any foods reacting to the iodine test are likely to cause IBS. However, I will list the vegetables that, when cooked, are given the following ratings:

0 – no starch
Tr – a trace of starch
0.1 – the most I could recommend as a safe amount

---

*My testing with iodine disagrees with this result.

Try them for yourself and if you find any of these foods bring on a return of symptoms, eliminate them.

This information was taken from the fifth supplement to McCance & Widdowson's *The Composition of Foods* (fourth edition). Unless otherwise stated, all were tested, boiled in salted water.

Vegetable	Starch content	Comments
Ackee	Tr	
Agar (dried)	0	
Amaranth leaves	0.1	
Artichoke, globe	Tr	
Artichoke, Jerusalem	Tr	
Asparagus	Tr	
Bamboo shoots (canned)	Tr	
Beetroot (pickled)	Tr	Boiled in salted water rates 0.7.
Broccoli	Tr	Frozen and boiled rates 0.8.
purple sprouting	0.1	
Cabbage	0.1	I cannot recommend
red cabbage	0.1	cabbage.
summer cabbage	0.1	
white cabbage	0.1	
Celery	Tr	
Chicory	0.1	
Courgette	0.1	
Curly kale	0.1	
Fennel, Florence	0.1	
Mushrooms (canned)	Tr	
Onions	Tr	I advise caution regarding
dried	Tr	the use of fresh onions,
pickled	Tr	despite the same rating
cocktail/silverskin	Tr	for dried. Caramelisation of fresh onions during frying may cause RS.
Peppers – red	0.1	Green peppers contain 0.2.

Petit pois peas	Tr	No other peas contain so little starch.
Pumpkin	0.1	Type of pumpkin is not specified.
Quorn	Tr	
Sauerkraut	Tr	Compare this to cabbage, above.
Sea kale	0	
Spinach (fresh)	Tr	Frozen spinach rates 0.2.
Swede	0.1	
Tomatoes, fried	0.1	
grilled	Tr	
juice	Tr	Canned rates 0.2 and tomato puree 0.3.
Turnip	0.1	
turnip tops	0.1	
Vine leaves	0.1	Preserved in brine.

9

What can I eat?

Now for the good news – and there's lots of it, despite the huge list of things we can't eat. The Sinclair Diet System is not another dreary, tasteless 'lettuce leaf and nut cutlet' regime. Many of our recipes are very sophisticated – even decadent! You might discover that food has never tasted better. You can skip this section if you like and go straight on to the recipe section, but there are some things you should know about the advantages of eating vegetables raw, because you are going to need to eat a lot of salads. To reassure yourself that the diet is not only delicious but also good for you, spend a few moments reading the following pages.

Raw vegetables are delicious and better for you

Most vegetables contain starch – even when raw. But when eaten raw, the small amount of starch passes through the digestive system, sealed in the vegetable cell. (There are two exceptions to this rule – cauliflower and avocado.)

One reference source* explains it thus:

> Uncooked starchy foods are not easy to digest because the starch granules are contained within the cell walls of the plant which the digestive juices cannot easily penetrate. Cooking softens the cell walls and allows water to enter the starch granules causing them to disintegrate and gelatinize.

At first glance this extract would seem to say that raw vegetables are less easy to digest than cooked – and this is true for people with a normal digestion. However, for those of us

---

*Food Science, Nutrition and Health, fifth edition, by Brian A. Fox and Allan G. Cameron, published by Edward Arnold, 1992.

with starch-intolerance IBS, the fact that the starch granules stay locked within the cell walls when the vegetable is in a raw state means that we can eat these foods safely.

Doctors advise that people who have trouble digesting fibre (which is what the cell wall is composed of) should remember to chew foods well. I have discovered, however, that the elimination of starch in my diet has reduced my sensitivity to indigestion. In the past, I frequently suffered from heart-burn and belching after meals – now I experience no discomfort after eating salads and raw vegetables.

When the vegetable is cooked, the starch in the vegetable is also cooked, producing RS (resistant starch). This is another reason why starchy vegetables when cooked may cause IBS symptoms in those of us who are starch-intolerant.

When buying and preparing your salad vegetables, remember that the cell walls become weaker as the vegetables become stale and flabby. To ensure the best possible digestibility, eat your salads when they are as fresh as possible. Serve them as whole as possible and prepare them just before the meal. Always use sharp kitchen knives – there is evidence to show that more vitamin C is lost when vegetables are cut with a blunt knife than a sharp one, presumably because a blunt knife ruptures more vegetable cells by crushing.

Vitamins are lost when vegetables are cooked

One of the major disadvantages of cooking vegetables, even for people with normal digestion, is that much of their important vitamin content is lost during cooking, either because they are destroyed by heat or because they are lost in the cooking water. These are known as the water-soluble vitamins. All are needed by your body every day, but your body is unable to store them longer than a day at a time because any left over from you daily needs are excreted in your urine. For this reason you need to eat them every day.

Green leafy vegetables, tomatoes, and fruit contain small amounts of vitamins B1 and B2, and larger amounts of another B vitamin, niacin, all of which are in danger of being lost in cooking. But they are a major source of one of the most important water-soluble vitamins – ascorbic acid, or vitamin

C. On the Sinclair Diet System you'll be eating most of your vegetables raw and will be getting good supplies of vitamin C daily.

The importance of proteins

Although the Sinclair Diet System has to eliminate so many starch foods, it is rich in protein, and protein foods are the most important part of the dietary needs of everyone.

People who are allergic to proteins (they are very few) are in desperate trouble and can develop serious illnesses, because proteins build and maintain every cell of the body and enable everything to work properly. We could not live without protein.

In case you do not know what the main sources of protein are, here is a list, showing the most important sources in descending order:

- Eggs.
- Milk and milk products.
- Liver and other glandular meats.
- Muscle meats.
- Fish and fowl.
- Yeast.
- Wheatgerm.
- Soy flour.
- Some nuts.

Because proteins in cereal grains, legumes and most nuts lack some of the essential amino acids, they are of value as proteins only when eaten with eggs, milk or meat, or with each other, so that all essential acids are provided in the diet. This is why in a normal diet, breakfast cereals are eaten with milk, toast is buttered, cakes are made with eggs/butter/milk, and so on.

Most people in Western countries get sufficient protein from a normal diet, but people recovering from illnesses or going on a weight-loss diet should increase their intake.

If your diet until now has been a low-protein diet, consisting mainly of refined carbohydrates, the Sinclair Diet System, apart from eliminating IBS symptoms, should boost your energy levels and feeling of well-being.

The Sinclair Diet System – safe foods

All protein foods

Beef, lamb, pork, poultry, game, fish, eggs, milk, cheese, butter, cream, cottage cheese, yoghurt, crème fraîche, fromage frais.

All vegetables raw
The exceptions are cauliflower and avocado. Tomatoes, which are really a kind of berry, are closer to a fruit and can be eaten lightly cooked and as tomato juice. As tomato paste, they may cause problems – refer to the recipe section (page 73). Olives, also a berry, can be eaten cooked.

All fruits, fresh, cooked, canned or dried
The exceptions are bananas and rhubarb (which is a vegetable, not a fruit).

Dried foods
Onions, garlic and herbs.

Spices
Use in moderation – test before using or refer to the section listing the starch content of herbs and spices. Cocoa (which is a berry) may be eaten or drunk.

Fresh and dried herbs
Use cooked or raw. Refer to my notes in the section listing the starch content of herbs and spices (pages 44–5).

Savoury dishes
Safe dishes include: roasted, grilled, boiled, baked, poached, scalloped, casseroled, stewed and braised meats, poultry, fish and eggs, seasoned with dried onion or garlic, mustard, fresh or cooked fruits, herbs, wine, cream, sauces thickened with cream, crème fraîche, yoghurt, butter. All cooked meats such as ham, pastrami, corned beef, chicken, turkey, bacon. All starch-free processed meat, poultry and fish products such as European sausages, pepperoni, salami, liver sausage and some pâtés. All canned fish such as salmon, tuna, herrings, kippers, unless in a sauce containing starch. Uncoated frozen fish. All types of

salads made from any combination of raw vegetables, herbs, fruits, cheese, eggs, fish, poultry and meats.

Sweet dishes
Safe dishes include: ice cream, mousse, fruit yoghurts, egg custards, brûlées, custard sauces, meringues, cooked and fresh fruit, fruit sauces, toffees, fudge, chocolates, cakes and biscuits made with ground almonds.

If you think that the list of what you can't eat is longer than what you can eat – don't be downhearted! Turn to the recipe section.

Beverages
One cheery footnote – coffee, tea, wine, spirits, beer and lager can all be part of the Sinclair Diet System. Although whisky, bourbon and vodka are distilled from grains, the iodine test shows that they do not contain starch. Some beers are made with rice, and all are made with hops, but they also do not seem to contain starch when tested. I haven't tested every brand on the market. If you are worried, test a small amount before you drink.

Most soft drinks are starch-free, but beware of lemon barley water, which if made correctly, contains barley flour. You should also be cautious about malted milk shakes and milk drinks which contain malt extract – test before drinking. Strong drinks could cause problems.

I have recently discovered that orange juice in cardboard packs contains starch. Most paper and cardboard (except coffee filters) contain a great deal of starch, and I suppose that in the case of orange juice, the acid in the juice permeates the wax lining, allowing small amounts of starch to come through. This may not affect you unless you are extremely starch intolerant, but it is wise to be aware of the problem. Milk does not appear to be affected.

Fruit juices and hot drinks used to be painful to drink before I eliminated starch. I have come to the conclusion that my intolerance to starch had so aggravated my digestive tract that acidic and hot drinks caused pain. Now it is blissfully calm.

Medicines

Most tablets and pills – including herbal pills and vitamins – contain starch and cannot be included in the Sinclair Diet System in their present form. Homeopathic pills contain only minute amounts of starch and you may be able to continue taking these. If symptoms recur you will have to eliminate them. (I understand that liquid versions of homeopathic remedies are available through homeopathic practitioners.)

It will probably be quite frightening to contemplate giving up the very medicines you feel are the only thing keeping you going. These will usually be pain relievers such as paracetamol or aspirin-based medications, laxatives and perhaps tranquillisers.

You may, however, find that the medication you are taking is available in liquid or starch-free formulation: Merbentyl, for example, a muscle relaxant often prescribed for IBS, is available in liquid form.

If you are taking any tranquillisers, it is *essential* that you consult your doctor before trying to give up.

Pain relievers

These are available in liquid or starch-free forms. Ask your doctor to prescribe them or buy Aspro-clear or Alka-seltzer from your chemist or supermarket.

Vitamin pills

There are now some vitamin capsules that do not contain starch. Always read the list of ingredients, and if in doubt, ask your chemist. Many vitamin supplements are available in liquid form.

Laxatives

If you regularly take laxatives, Epsom salts (which I take on the advice of a specialist at St Mark's Hospital, London) contain no starch and are excellent and non habit-forming. It is an old-fashioned remedy which lost favour when new 'improved' drugs and herbal pills became available. Most of these, however, have proved habit-forming and many doctors are now returning to Epsom salts.

The correct chemical name for Epsom salts is magnesium sulphate. Magnesium is one of the minerals essential for good health. If you want to reassure yourself about this much neglected mineral – which has many other health-promoting properties, including helping premenstrual tension, muscle cramps, fatigue and lowering high blood pressure in women – refer to *Nutritional Medicine* by Dr Stephen Davies and Dr Alan Stewart, published by Pan Books. Magnesium is also available as Milk of Magnesia and as various magnesium tablets – just make sure they're starch-free.

Examples of my daily diet

These are the sort of things I eat every day, whether at home or out. The Sinclair Diet System doesn't allow for lazy shopping – you have to have more in the cupboard than a loaf of bread and a pack of butter.

Breakfast
Orange juice, starch-free yoghurt, cooked or raw fruit, coffee or tea, bacon, starch-free sausages (usually German), scrambled, poached, boiled or fried eggs, turkey rashers, fried apple rings, a 'Dutch' breakfast consisting of a boiled egg, mild cheese and salami.

I must confess my breakfast is usually only orange juice, coffee and yoghurt but I *could* eat all the rest on the diet. Recently on holiday in America, while everyone else was having pancakes with maple syrup, I discovered that scrambled eggs with maple syrup tastes almost as good. After all, scrambled eggs are just pancakes with the flour left out!

Lunch
Cheese, ham, pastrami, salmon, tuna, left-over cold chicken from last night's supper or cottage cheese with salad or an apple. Simple hot dishes such as 'Bacon Star' and 'Italian Salmon Bake' (see recipe section) or an omelette. McDonald's cheeseburgers and salad. Yoghurt, cooked or raw fruit, ice cream, meringue, cake or biscuits made from ground almonds, coffee or tea, fruit juice.

Supper

Meat, chicken or fish, braised, roasted, fried, grilled or casseroled without cooked fresh vegetables but with dried onion, dried garlic, herbs, tomatoes, wine, mustard, lemon juice, fruit. Salad – coleslaw or green salad or mixtures of both. Ice cream, yoghurt, mousse, jelly, chocolates, meringues, egg custards such as crème brûlée, crème caramel, cakes, biscuits and desserts made with ground almonds, cooked or canned fruit or fresh fruit salad with cream.

Snacks

Yoghurt, cheese, cold meats, pâté with tomato, pepperoni, fruit dried, cooked or raw, dates and cream cheese, cheese and lettuce, cakes and biscuits made with ground almonds, chocolate or sweets.

10

Is the Sinclair Diet System nutritionally safe?

Is there enough fibre?
– wholegrains are not the whole truth

'Fibre' has become the buzz word of the nutritional world. Everyone is encouraged to eat more of it to be healthy. Unfortunately, most people (including some doctors) seem to have the impression that fibre is found only in wholegrains and bran – all those TV adverts showing plates laden with 'healthy eating' breakfast cereals have been very persuasive!

For years the standard treatment for IBS has been to put the patient on a high-fibre diet which has usually meant primarily wholegrains and bran. The results have been dismal. I don't know how many tonnes of bran and wholegrains I have munched through, clutching my stomach in agony at the same time.

We certainly need fibre – most of us have such sluggardly guts that we need all the help we can get. We need fibre to provide the bulk that helps push everything through the bowel and to retain the necessary water that keeps stools soft, preventing the hard stools that result in constipation. But bran and wholegrain fibre is not the answer for those of us who are starch-intolerant. And it may not even be the answer for people with normal digestion.

Bran is the outside skin of wholegrains. The most commonly extracted bran is from wheat. There are two disadvantages of bran – both of eating it after extraction and of eating it on the wholegrain or in wholemeal bread:

- It contains a substance called *phytic acid which blocks the absorption of calcium, magnesium, iron, zinc, copper and vitamin B6 –all of which you need daily.

- Because it is the outside skin of the grain, bran contains a high percentage of the chemicals sprayed on the crop – chemicals that we can't wash off at home. And none of us wants to eat more of those than we have to.

By far the best form of fibre to eat – whether you're an IBS sufferer or not – is the fibre from green vegetables and fruit, and the Sinclair Diet System is rich in this fibre. *Fruit and vegetable fibre provides you with large quantities of vitamins A, B, C and E, magnesium and a wide range of other minerals. All the lovely salads and fresh fruit you're going to begin eating will improve your overall health as well as eliminating your IBS symptoms.

What about the cholesterol monster?

The Sinclair Diet System has two advantages for people worried about cholesterol levels.

- It is now known that fruit and vegetable fibre is better (than bran or grain fibre) at lowering blood cholesterol levels. Higher consumptions of vegetables and fruit are associated with a lower risk of coronary heart disease.
- Because you now won't be eating all the high-starch foods made with butter or margarine (and many margarines are cholesterol culprits) such as cakes, pastries, pancakes and puddings – and because you won't be eating buttered bread, toast, rolls, scones or buns, or deep-fried fish and chips – your intake of fatty foods will automatically be lowered.

If you're worried that eliminating high-starch foods means you may tend to eat more high-caloried foods such as meat, cheese, ice cream and yoghurt, there are low-fat types of all these foods now available. But once again a word of warning: remember to look at the ingredients on the packs of low-fat foods. Many manufacturers tend to thicken skim-milk products such as yoghurts or ice cream with modified starch.

---

*From *The Vitality Diet* by Maryon Stewart and Dr Alan Stewart, published by Optima in 1992.

What if you're vegetarian?

The Sinclair Diet System is extremely difficult for people who don't eat some meat or fish. A vegetarian diet is usually full of bread and grain products and it's difficult enough for vegetarians at the best of times to keep up their protein levels without eating lots of beans and lentils – foods which are, unfortunately, among the worst offenders for starch-intolerant IBS sufferers.

If you feel from the symptoms I've described that eliminating starch would help you, you will have to eat large amounts of fruit and raw vegetables and a serving of cheese or eggs at every meal.

However, vegans will find it almost impossible to get enough of the right foods to sustain good health. Tofu (bean curd) is worth trying as it contains only small amounts of starch. Quorn and TVP are too starchy. If you are experiencing IBS symptoms badly, I would recommend a week's trial of the first stage of the Sinclair Diet System and if you experience relief of symptoms, then you may be able to work out a satisfactory diet without bread and lentils – but it will not be easy.

11

The side-effects of a starch-free diet

Most modern nutritionists say that 60 per cent of our diet should be carbohydrate. While I do not argue with this, it was only a few years ago that nutritionists were advising a diet with a far higher proportion of protein.

The high-starch grain and root foods which are now such a large part of our diet are quite new in evolutionary terms. When our ancestors were hunter-gatherers they lived on wild plants, honey and animals. It was only when humans learned to grow their own food, enabling them to give up their nomadic lifestyles and become farmers, that grain and root crops, previously eaten only in small amounts, became commonly eaten. Grains, which could be stored and eaten for most of the year, were seen as being especially useful, but meat and wild plants continued to be a major part of the diet for many centuries.

The Industrial Revolution, which mechanised the milling and refining of flour, made bread relatively cheap and easily produced, enormously increasing the intake of starch in the average diet, while at the same time reducing the quality of the carbohydrates eaten.

There is still some scientific controversy over whether or not we are adapted to eat large quantities of starch. All the disaccharides (sucrose, lactose and maltose) and the polysaccharides (starch) became widely eaten in human diet only after people became agriculturists. Sucrose, the ordinary sugar we now eat in such abundance, was almost unknown in Shakespeare's time and until as recently as the middle of the nineteenth century was so expensive that only the rich could afford it. Honey and fructose, the easily digested simple sugar found in fruit, have been eaten by humans from prehistoric times.

In general, the human digestion is very flexible. The variety and range of different diets eaten all around the world is enormous. In Western societies as recently as the Middle Ages, for example, people ate mostly meat and bread and very little in the way of green vegetables. Not long ago the Eskimo diet was originally almost entirely protein and fat, being mostly fish and blubber.

The Sinclair Diet System includes almost no carbohydrates except for sugars, and is therefore unbalanced by today's recommended standards. However, I survive very well and am generally in very good health. It is probably quite similar to the diet of our hunter-gatherer ancestors, being mainly meat or other proteins and raw plants (except that I haven't included any recipes for Woolly Mammoth stew). But the Sinclair Diet System does cause side-effects – both good and bad.

First the good news

One of the surprising and welcome side-effects I have noticed is that I now rarely feel the cold. As a child I used to suffer from bad circulation in cold weather – my music teacher always had to give me five minutes of hand exercises before I could begin to play the piano. Chilblains were agony every winter. Even as an adult, I once developed early stages of gangrene in one of my toes because of a lack of blood. Now I notice that I feel quite warm when others around me are huddled into thick clothes and are complaining of feeling chilly. Perhaps I've discovered the secret of the Eskimos' ability to withstand the cold.

I also now have none of the joint pains that plagued me since childhood. My elbows, finger joints and knees were always aching – 'growing pains' was the usual diagnosis. The pains continued long after I'd grown, but I became resigned to them and sought refuge in hot baths and hot-water bottles. It was not until a few months after I had begun eliminating starch that I noticed that as I was sitting in front of the TV at night, I was no longer rubbing my aching knees and elbows. They weren't aching.

Some doctors now believe that rheumatoid arthritis symptoms may be eliminated by giving up wheat and gluten. As an adult I never sought help for my joint pains and consequently was never diagnosed as having rheumatoid arthritis, so I can't claim to have been cured from it, but I now rarely ever suffer from joint pains.

Now the bad news

One disadvantage of the Sinclair Diet System (apart from the obvious ones!) is that carbohydrates are the 'tranquillisers' of the food world and make you feel calmer. Eliminating all except sugar can make you irritable, especially when you're hungry and particularly in the early stages of the diet when your body is still unused to going without starch. Be prepared to eat immediately you get that empty feeling, otherwise you may behave like a hungry baby and begin screaming at people.

If you also suffer from hypoglycaemia

You will probably already have experienced faintness and confusion when you're hungry – even on a normal diet. Hypoglycaemia or low blood sugar is caused by a deficiency of glucose in the bloodstream (all carbohydrates have to be broken down by the digestive system to be turned into glucose). The moment you feel the symptoms of low blood sugar, you need food immediately. If bread and starchy foods make up a large part of your diet, you may find that when you first give them up, you will experience headaches, weakness, faintness, even panic attacks. In fact, you may not even be aware until then that you suffer from hypoglycaemia – it is often undiagnosed for years.

Because glucose is the sole source of energy for the brain, a deficiency of glucose will cause these symptoms often before you even know you're hungry. Other symptoms can range from irritability, nausea, fast heartbeat, anxiety, cold sweats and even vertigo, to behaviour problems and mood swings.

For many years doctors have been advising patients to eat a quick carbohydrate meal to boost their low blood sugar levels. However, recent medical thinking on this problem has changed. I quote from *Nutritional Medicine* by Dr Stephen Davies and Dr Alan Stewart, published by Pan Books:

> One of the commonest contributing factors in hypoglycae-mia in the West is excessive refined carbohydrate consump-tion.... Some doctors are under the misconception that if a person has a low blood sugar they should simply have a cup of tea with a few teaspoonfuls of sugar. This is wrong. Whilst

this might well produce relief of the symptoms for a while, it encourages a vicious circle; a low blood sugar, refined carbohydrate ingestion, excessive insulin secretion, followed by a low blood sugar. One approach to treatment of low blood sugar is the elimination of refined carbohydrates from the diet.

Other writers on the subject recommend eating more meat, fish, eggs, cheese and vegetables, and stress the long-term importance of a low-refined-carbohydrate, high-protein diet (see *Let's Get Well*, by Adelle Davis, published by Unwin Paperbacks, 1979).

As an IBS sufferer, your problems are doubled if you also suffer from low blood sugar, because when hungry you need food instantly. One of the greatest difficulties of the Sinclair Diet System is that when you're out, you can't grab a quick sandwich. Read the chapter on eating out and learn which fast foods are safe.

You must make sure you eat regular, frequent meals – don't wait until you feel hunger-pangs. It's better to eat six small meals a day than three large ones. Make cakes, biscuits, candies and sweets with honey and fruit sugar from the baking recipes in this book and carry them with you if you're travelling, or take cheese segments, dried or fresh fruit, almonds and sliced meats. I usually make sure I have several small packets of raisins in my bag when I'm travelling. You never know when you're going to be stuck in a traffic jam or train hold-up.

12

Guide to eating out

Eating out at someone else's home is very difficult. Most people don't realise the number of foods that contain starch and it's embarrassing to have to lay down rules. Unless you've been invited to your nearest and dearest's house for dinner, you may find it better to confess your problem and bring your own food or suggest that you arrive after the meal.

Eating at a party is not quite so problematic – there's sure to be something on the table you can nibble at to stave off hunger pangs. Be prepared not to be able to eat much. I usually eat something at home before I go so that I can last the distance.

You'll be glad to hear that most restaurants have some dishes on their menus that can be eaten on the Sinclair Diet System, such as grilled meats, poultry, fish with raw salad (no cooked vegetables, beans or potato salad) followed by fruit, ice cream, mousse or crème brûlée, etc. If you fancy a meat or fish dish cooked in sauce, ask the waiter to find out if it contains flour or cornflour. If you're very careful, you can pick your way through a pizza by eating only the topping – eliminating any cooked vegetables such as peppers. But sad to say, the most convenient fast foods – those that we rely on most often such as fish and chips or anything cooked in batter – are out of the question.

Who's out

Chinese

Of course rice is out and even wok-cooked vegetables are a problem. Chinese cooking also includes lots of soy sauce (made from lentils) and modified starch in the form of cornflour.

Indian

Rice is the worst offender again, and although Indian curries are usually cooked without starch thickening (they use mostly yoghurt), inevitably fresh onions or garlic will have been browned causing RS, and many of the spices are very starchy.

The local chippy

No fish and chips – sorry! But if your local chippy sells fried chicken, providing it has no batter, you can eat that – without chips.

Who's not recommended

Pizza parlours

Unless you're very careful and eat only the pizza topping. Tomato paste or purée used on the pizza can be a problem as this contains low but unacceptable levels of starch to those of us who can only tolerate the very lowest starch rating. Also some tomato sauces contain modified starch. I have eaten pizza toppings in the past, although I really don't think it worthwhile nowadays. But pizza parlours now often have very good salads which are a complete meal, although you'll have to give up the pasta.

Vegetarian

Unless you eat only raw dishes.

Teashops and coffee bars

These are not easy. Most of the food choices are sandwiches, filled rolls, cakes and pastries. Sometimes you can buy raw salads or yoghurts (look carefully at the ingredients on the pack). You may have to settle for cheese segments or an ice cream sundae.

Who's in

McDonald's

Contrary as it may sound, McDonald's is such a life-saver for those of us who can't eat starch that it's top of my list. If you've always associated McDonald's with the dreaded description 'junk food', think again. Their latest nutritional analysis compares favourably with those of similar foods in *The Composition of Foods*. And best of all, they don't change the ingredients. That may sound like a gourmet's nightmare, but for those of us who have to know what our food contains, at McDonald's you always know exactly what you're getting, regardless of where you are. They're not suddenly going to bulk up their burger patties with breadcrumbs or thicken their thickshakes with modified starch. All over the world, McDonald's food is made to the same recipes and they have very strict specifications about the quality and consistency of their ingredients.

All McDonald's hamburgers are made from 100 per cent meat and are safe for us to eat on the Sinclair Diet System. Of course, we can't eat the bun, but we can eat the burger inside.

I recommend the cheeseburger – it's easily removed from the bun (wear your glasses as you must make sure no little pieces of bread stick to the burger) and slim enough to fold over and eat with the sticky sauce and cheese inside, like a sandwich. The cheese and the tomato sauce contain no starch, and I've never found the gherkin slice to cause me any problems, although this can be easily discarded.

McDonald's also have excellent salads these days, but be careful about the packaged dressings. Most are starch-free but at least one variety has modified starch. They do, however, have a full list of ingredients on the pack. McDonald's thickshakes are made from skimmed milk, cream and various other flavourings and stabilisers, but they contain no starch thickening. Their ice cream sundaes are also starch-free, and so are the sauces – except the fudge sauce.

The plain Hamburger, the Quarter Pounder and the Quarter Pounder with Cheese are safe to eat (although the Quarter Pounder is a little chunky to fold over). But the Big Mac is out – the sauce contains modified starch – and so is the Quarter

Pounder with Cheese Deluxe, which includes a mayonnaise with modified starch.

All their beverages are starch-free but none of their other food is suitable. I suggest you ask for a copy of their 'Nutritional Information' guide, which lists the ingredients of all their foods.

If you'd told me years ago that I would gaze with delight on the familiar McDonald's sign, I would never have believed you. But when you're tired and hungry and scared to try unfamiliar food, those golden arches are like a magnet! A cheeseburger and a thickshake makes a good snack; two cheeseburgers, a salad and a thickshake make a meal; two cheeseburgers, a salad, a thickshake and a sundae is a feast!

Other fast-food chains may have starch-free food, but I am not aware of any. Burger King's hamburgers, for example, are 100 per cent beef, but their mayonnaise, ketchup and Cheddar cheese fillings contain modified starch. Their milk shakes and ice creams, however, are starch-free.

Cafes

Fried eggs, poached eggs, scrambled eggs, bacon, grilled tomatoes. Don't eat the sausages or toast.

Pubs

Order a plain steak or a ploughman's (just leave the bread roll, the pickled onion and the chutney). Beware of potato salad, beetroot and cooked cold vegetables in the salad.

Steakhouses

Best to order a plain steak *without* chips, roast, new or jacket potatoes. Pepper steak is fine unless it has a sauce which may be thickened with flour or cornflour.

French/Italian/Greek/English restaurants

Order carefully and ask the waiter to help. If the restaurant values its reputation it will be happy to tell you what each dish contains. Most cream or wine sauces cooked by good chefs are made without cornflour or flour – see the recipe section for the correct methods of making cream and wine sauces. There's usually a no-starch dessert on the menu, such as ice cream, sorbet, mousse, crème brûlée, crème caramel (the caramelisation of the sugar in both the crème brûlée and the crème caramel may cause problems for some).

13

Start shopping

Pack identification

The first thing to remember when you're buying canned, chilled, frozen or processed foods of any kind is to read the back of the pack – every pack. Become a connoisseur of that list of ingredients. It's surprising where and how often modified starch is used, and regrettably, it's on the increase.

A huge range of foods must, of necessity, contain wheat flour or modified starch and you'll quickly learn which they are. But in many cases, modified starch is entirely unnecessary as a recipe ingredient. It's used simply to make foods cheaper to produce. Many bought oil and vinegar dressings contain modified starch, especially in France, the home of the vinaigrette – don't ask me why! Canned soups always contain modified starch. Some mayonnaises contain modified starch, some do not. Some yoghurts do, some don't. Fruit and chocolate fudge sauce or ripples in some ice creams usually contain modified starch. Even foods to which you would not add thickening if you were making it in your own home – such as baby foods, lemon curd, chutneys, etc. – often contain starch when they're commercially prepared.

14

Recipes

- All the recipes are in the very low-to-no-starch category and can be eaten at any stage of the diet.
- If you are still in the early stages of elimination, add servings of potatoes, rice or cooked vegetables.
- Your family and friends will also enjoy these recipes. Just add servings of pasta, rice, bread or cooked vegetables for people with normal digestion.

Starch-free cooking with the Sinclair Diet System is just as easy as everyday cooking, but there are some new rules. Apart from eliminating the obvious forms of starch as already discussed, many of the processed convenience foods you've used in the past such as stock cubes or Gravox, Bisto, Marmite and Bovril should not be used in our diet as they all contain starch of some sort. Many spices should also be avoided, either fresh or raw. Ginger, for example, one of the most delicious additions to spicy foods, is a root and very starchy, even as a powder. Cinnamon, a bark, also contains starch. But there are plenty of ways to 'beef' up the taste of your food – in fact, you'll discover a whole new range of lovely flavours.

According to my testing, herbs do not contain starch, either raw or cooked, and I find them a valuable addition to many dishes. Mustard is also starch-free according to the iodine test, and available in so many different flavour variations that you'll find it a great standby. I always have at least three varieties on hand to use in different ways instead of stock cubes.

The Sinclair Diet System store cupboard

This should contain:

Dried garlic granules Sometimes called garlic powder, this is milder than fresh garlic but with a very good flavour. Do not confuse this with *garlic salt*. Garlic granules and garlic salt look very alike and often the packaging is so similar that it's easy to mistake one for the other. But garlic salt is *so* salty that you'll soon know the difference if you add it by mistake – the food will be inedible.

Dried onion flakes   These are milder than fresh onions and not so delicious, but a reasonably good substitute.

Dried onion granules   These are stronger than fresh onions. Use only a little.

Dried herbs   Experiment with the various types of mixed herbs now available, such as Italian, Mediterranean, Provence, etc. They are often freeze-dried and have a very good flavour.

Fresh herbs   The greatest flavour enhancer, and you can use them in so many dishes. Buy them planted in pots if you can, as they stay fresh longer. If you grow your own, so much the better!

Lemons   A drop or two is wonderful for bringing out the flavour of foods. A good trick is to pierce the lemon with a fine skewer or thick darning needle and just squeeze out the juice when you need it. This way it stays fresh far longer.

Fruit jellies   Try jelly jams such as red currant, blackberry, quince and strawberry. The best brand is Wilkins & Sons' 'Tiptrees' – not always readily available, but look for it in good supermarkets and speciality stores. All of these are wonderful with hot or cold meats (yes, even the strawberry!). You can also mix them with mustard for a very good substitute for chutney, or simply add a dab of mustard and a dab of jelly to the plate, and eat them both at the same time.

Honey   This is easier for people with IBS symptoms to digest than sugar, and can be used in so many ways, both in sweet and savoury dishes.

Fruit sugar (proper name 'fructose')   Various brands are on the market, but the most readily available is 'Dietade' Fruit Sugar.

Ground almond   This is the best starch-free substitute for flour that I have found. It is not really like flour in any way, except that it can look and taste quite like flour. Ground almond makes good cakes or biscuits, although you won't be able to use it for light sponges or breads or sauces.

Mustards   I use mustard frequently because it can replace flavours and spices that have had to be eliminated. *The Composition of Foods* gives mustard powder and seeds various ratings, ranging from N, which means that starch is present in significant quantities but there is no reliable information on the amount, to 1.9 and 0.3. It does not give any information about the brands of mustard that were tested to get these results. As I am unable to detect any starch in the brands and types that I use, and as I use mustard so often, an explanatory note is in order:

Guide to mustards

Mustard is produced from the seeds of three different types of plants, giving white (or yellow) mustard, black mustard and brown mustard. The most commonly known in this country are either English mustards made from white seeds and sold as a dry powder or a paste, and French and German mustards, which are usually in paste form, mixed with wine or vinegar. American mustards, generally very mild, are beginning to become popular.

English mustards usually contain wheat flour, whether powder or paste, and I avoid them. It may be that these are the mustards tested in *The Composition of Foods*. Genuine French (Dijon), German or American mustards, however, usually do not contain any starch additives, although you should check the list of ingredients. You may see included in the list, 'mustard flour', which is, in fact, ground mustard seed and not wheat flour, and therefore is safe to eat.

All types of mustard can be used in the Sinclair Diet System, ranging from the sweet honey-mustards to the salty, savoury flavour of Greek mustard with black olives. The largest variety by far are the Dijon mustards which come in a range of colours and types, either smooth or whole seed (coarse grain). The seeds are sometimes peppercorns and sometimes mustard seeds – either is fine to eat.

The honey-mustard I often include in recipes is usually 'Honeycup', a Canadian brand – very mild and sweet and an excellent addition to savoury sauces and gravies because it helps replace the sweetish/savoury flavour of vegetables. There are other brands of honey-mustards on the market and you can make your own substitute by mixing a good Dijon mustard with honey to taste.

Greek mustard with black olives is good for adding a deeper taste to meat dishes – a bit like Marmite. It must be used with caution as it has quite a strong flavour.

Soups

Soups are among the most difficult dishes to include on a starch-free diet. Most soups contain starch whether they're made from meat and vegetable stocks or cream sauces. The range is therefore very limited for those of us with starch intolerance.

You will see I have included several made with tomatoes. I feel I should add a warning note at this point: I can't make up my mind about tomatoes – not the taste, which I love, but whether they contain enough starch to worry about.

Tomatoes are properly classified as a fruit and therefore should not contain starch. I've tested them in a number of ways – lightly grilled, lightly fried, cooked for an hour or so, cooked with liquid and without. Sometimes they show evidence of starch, sometimes not. Surprisingly, the less ripe they are, the less starch is in evidence – which is the opposite of bananas!

I was very confused about tomatoes for a long time, but if you look at the list of vegetables in chapter 8, you'll see the answer: according to *The Composition of Foods*, tomato juice, tomatoes raw and grilled contain only a trace of starch, fried (in corn oil) they contain 0.1, canned they contain 0.2 and puréed they contain 0.3. This indicates to me that the more they are cooked, the more starch they develop. Obviously, therefore, if you use tomato purée or canned tomatoes in a recipe, you are already beginning from a higher starch basis and the longer you cook the tomatoes, the more starchy they may become. I would recommend therefore, that fresh tomatoes or tomato juice be used, although a very small amount of tomato ketchup has never caused me any trouble.

I leave it to you to decide. If you begin to experience IBS symptoms after eating dishes with a large cooked tomato content, give them up. Any symptoms you may experience will not be dramatically bad, and this will all depend on how intolerant you are to starch. Raw tomatoes are, of course, completely safe.

I have also included a recipe for asparagus soup because it contains only a trace of starch when cooked from fresh. Frozen, it contains too much starch.

Chicken and apple soup

Ingredients   **Serves four**

2 *chicken breasts with bones and skin*
3 *teaspoons chopped fresh rosemary*
3 *teaspoons clear honey*
4 *tablespoons olive oil*
3 *teaspoons garlic granules*
juice half a lemon
1.1 litres (2 pints) water
1 *teaspoon honey-mustard*
½ *teaspoon olive mustard (optional)*
1 *teaspoon starch-free steak seasoning (optional)*
2 *sweet apples*
1 *tablespoon chopped parsley*

Method

Mix together the rosemary, honey, oil, lemon juice and 2 teaspoons of the garlic granules and marinate the chicken breasts in this mixture overnight (or instead, substitute two Marks & Spencer's rosemary/garlic marinaded chicken breasts).

Simmer the marinaded chicken breasts in the water for several hours until so tender that the meat is falling off the bones. Remove the chicken, extract the bones and discard.

Dice the meat and return it to the stock. Peel and grate the apples and add to the stock. Add the remaining teaspoon garlic powder, mustards and steak seasoning. Bring to the boil and simmer for 30 minutes. Check the flavour – more honey-mustard may be added if desired – and serve with chopped parsley.

Tomato and salmon soup

Ingredients   **Makes five bowls**

1 litre (36 fl oz) tomato juice
50 g (2 oz) butter
½ *teaspoon garlic powder*
pinch onion powder
3 *teaspoons fruit sugar*
1 *teaspoon lemon juice*
105 g (4 oz) can pink salmon with juice
cream and chopped parsley to garnish

Method

Process the tomato juice, salmon, garlic and onion powder in food blender until almost smooth but not quite. Pour into a saucepan over a low heat. Add the fruit sugar, salt and black pepper, butter and lemon juice. Stir gently until hot, adjusting seasonings to taste.

Serve with a swirl of cream and a sprinkle of chopped parsley.

Sotos's lemon fish soup/stew

To turn this into a really filling meal, add a grilled round of goat's cheese or Haloumi cheese to each bowl.

Ingredients   **Serves four**
  425 ml (¾ pint) *water*
  425 ml (¾ pint) *apple juice*
  100 ml (4 fl oz) *homemade chicken stock (see 'Handy Hints' on*
      page 274)
  1 tablespoon dried onion flakes
  2 teaspoons dried garlic granules
  1 teaspoon honey-mustard
  juice of 1 lemon
  bunch coriander, oregano or parsley
  salt and pepper to taste
  4 good-sized portions of cod or haddock steaks, frozen or fresh
  more lemon juice to taste
  2–3 tablespoons chopped parsley
  Parmesan cheese

Method

Frozen fish should be defrosted before use. Chop the herbs, then combine all except the last four ingredients and bring to boil. Simmer for about an hour.

Wash the fish, remove any bones and add to the stock. Simmer for about 10–15 minutes or until the fish is cooked. Check the flavour, add more salt, pepper or lemon juice to taste.

Remove the fish, place it in a large serving dish, pour the soup over, then sprinkle with chopped parsley and Parmesan cheese.

Chilled cucumber and yoghurt soup

Ingredients   **Serves four**
550 g (1¼ lb) or 2 medium cucumbers, peeled, seeded and chopped
1 medium ripe pear, chopped
200 g (8 oz) carton low-fat plain yoghurt
325 ml (12 fl oz) water
100 ml (4 fl oz) homemade chicken stock jelly (see 'Handy Hints'
    on page 218)
4 tablespoons fresh basil leaves

Method
Blend or process all the ingredients until smooth. Cover and
refrigerate for several hours before serving. This soup can be
made up to two days ahead – store covered in the refrigerator.

Bouillabaisse

A genuine Mediterranean recipe which I have adapted – a meal
in itself.

Ingredients   **Serves four or five**
100 ml (4 fl oz) tablespoons olive oil
4 tablespoons dried onion flakes
1 teaspoon whole black or pink peppercorns
2 teaspoons garlic powder
500 g (1 lb) ripe tomatoes, peeled and chopped
½ teaspoon dried thyme or sprig fresh thyme
2 bayleaves
2 tablespoons orange juice
100 ml (4 fl oz) white wine
1.1 litres (2 pints) boiling water
salt
1 teaspoon honey-mustard or fruit sugar
1.5 kg (3 lb) fish

Method
Choose a selection of fish: conger or moray eel, gurnard, small
monkfish tail, red mullet, small bream, small bass, John Dory –
or if possible, Mediterranean varieties such as the spiny
scorpion fish called rascasse and other small rockfish, spiny

lobster, raw king prawns, scallops or calamari (ask your fishmonger to prepare any unfamiliar fish). Make sure the prawns are deveined but leave tails intact. Clean, cut and scale any unprepared fish.

Heat half the olive oil in large pan. Sauté the onions, garlic powder, bayleaves and peppercorns for a few seconds – don't allow to brown – then add the tomatoes and cook for 5 minutes.

Add the orange juice and thyme. Pour in the boiling water, increase the heat and stir well. Add the salt and rest of oil, boiling vigorously so that the oil is properly mixed. Add the wine, reduce the heat, taste and add sugar or honey-mustard if too tart.

Add the fish in order of cooking time – check with your fishmonger which will take the longest – and simmer for 5–8 minutes. Lift each fish out as it becomes cooked and place in a heated serving dish (leave some softer fish to disintegrate into the broth). Pour broth over fish and serve, or eat as two separate courses.

Creamy tomato and bacon soup

Ingredients   **Serves four**
500 g (1 lb) fresh tomatoes or 450 ml (16 fl oz) tomato juice
120 g (4 oz) diced bacon
100 ml (4 fl oz) water
1 teaspoon honey-mustard (optional)
1–2 teaspoons fruit sugar
$\frac{1}{2}$ teaspoon garlic granules
3 rounded tablespoons plain Greek yoghurt – either full- or
    low-fat
chopped chives

Method
Gently cook the bacon in a soup pot. When tender, add the tomatoes, water, honey-mustard, sugar and garlic granules. Bring slowly to the boil and simmer, adjusting seasonings. Stir in the yoghurt, bring to the boil again and serve, sprinkled with chopped chives.

Gazpacho

I have always loved this soup, but recently I discovered that the genuine Mediterranean recipe contains a slice or so of white bread, blended into the ingredients. This recipe, therefore, is an adaptation, and sadly I recommend that you ask the cook, before you eat the genuine article.

Ingredients **Serves three or four**

   2 *small green peppers, deseeded*
   1 kg (2¼ lb) ripe tomatoes, peeled and deseeded
   2 *small or 1 large cucumber, peeled*
   2 *garlic cloves, crushed*
   100 ml (4 fl oz) or less (to taste) best virgin olive oil
   about 6 tablespoons (or less) wine vinegar (to taste)
   salt
   1 teaspoon sugar

Method
Place the tomatoes in a bowl and pour boiling water over them, wait a few minutes then skewer each one with a fork and peel. Cut into chunks and remove the seeds.

   Put all the vegetables through a blender with the garlic. Add the olive oil, vinegar, salt and sugar. Blend to a light creamy consistency, adding a few tablespoons of iced water if necessary. Serve very cold accompanied by garnishes.

Garnishes
Dice 1 cucumber, 1 onion, 1 red pepper, 1 green pepper, 1 tomato and 2 boiled eggs finely and place in individual bowls so that a little of each can be sprinkled on the soup, as desired.

Cream of asparagus soup

Ingredients   **Serves four**
1 kg (2¼ lb) fresh asparagus (you can use just a few green tips and
    the bottom parts of the asparagus, cut into tiny pieces)
1.5 litres (2½ pints) water
100 ml (4 fl oz) homemade chicken stock jelly (see 'Handy Hints'
    on page 218)
1 egg yolk
125 ml (5 fl oz) crème fraîche
salt and freshly ground white pepper to taste

Method
Add the chicken stock to the water and blend well. Cut up the
asparagus stalks – if you have any suspicion that they may be
bitter, peel first – and cook them in the stock for 30 minutes.
Add the tips after 15 minutes.

Remove from the heat when they are all soft and puréed. If
the purée is not smooth enough, rub through a sieve. Combine
the egg yolk and crème fraîche, whisk into the purée, replace
over a very low heat just to heat through, adjust seasonings and
serve. May also be served cold.

Starters

Any of the dishes in this section can be served as starters or
party food, either together or individually. Serve the pâtés and
dips with raw vegetables for IBS people.

Asparagus gratin

Ingredients   **Serves two**
   500 g (1 lb) fresh asparagus
   100 g (4 oz) butter
   4–6 tablespoons grated Parmesan cheese
   salt and freshly ground pepper to taste

Method
Snap off the tough stems of the asparagus, peel the remainder
if needed, starting at the bottom and finishing 3–4 cm (1–1½
inches) from the tips, which should be left unpeeled.

Tie together in a bunch and cook standing up in boiling
water which should come about two-thirds of the way up the
asparagus, but should not cover the tips.

Cook for no longer than about 8–15 minutes, depending on
thickness. Remove and allow to drain. Place in a gratin dish,
melt the butter and pour over the asparagus, sprinkle over the
grated cheese and brown under a preheated grill.

Tapenade

Ingredients   **Makes one bowl**
   1 cup pitted black Spanish olives (in brine)
   ¼ cup capers
   6 anchovy fillets
   ⅓ cup canned tuna
   2 cloves garlic
   pinch ground bayleaves
   pinch dried thyme
   1 teaspoon mild Dijon mustard
   1 teaspoon cognac
   1 teaspoon lemon juice
   freshly ground black pepper
   4 tablespoons chopped parsley

Method
Drain the olives, capers, anchovy fillets and tuna. Peel the garlic. Put everything except the final four ingredients into an electric blender or food processor and purée. Stir in the cognac, lemon juice and parsley, season with black pepper to taste.

Gorgonzola mousse

Ingredients   **Serves six**
   6 eggs
   325 ml (12 fl oz) whipping cream
   1½ tablespoons (1½ sachets) gelatine
   4 tablespoons cold water
   375 g (13 oz) Gorgonzola cheese
   100 ml (4 fl oz) double cream
   light cooking oil

Method
Prepare a dish to use as a mould which should be at least 6.5 cm (3 inches) deep, by pouring in a small amount of cooking oil and tilting the dish so that the oil spreads over the base and around the sides. Set aside. Sieve or blend the cheese until smooth.

Separate the eggs, placing all the yolks in a saucepan or the top of a double boiler. Reserve 3 of the whites in a separate bowl. Put 6 tablespoons of the whipping cream into the saucepan with the egg yolks. Whisk the egg yolks and cream over simmering water until thick, then remove from the heat. Pour the gelatine into a small bowl, add the four tablespoons of cold water and stir over simmering water until the gelatine is dissolved. Remove from the heat. Pour the gelatine mixture into the egg and cream mixture and stir well. Add the sieved cheese to the egg/cream/gelatine mixture and leave to cool.

Meanwhile, beat the egg whites until stiff and set aside. In a separate bowl, beat the remaining whipping cream and the double cream together until stiff and set aside. Fold the beaten egg whites and the cheese mixture into the whipped cream mixture. Pour all into the prepared dish, making sure beforehand, that the oil still coats the sides. Chill in the refrigerator for at least 2 hours.

To unmould, upturn the dish onto a serving plate, wrap a tea-towel that has been dipped in hot water and wrung out, around the dish and wait for the mousse to slide out. This looks very good made in a square dish. Decorate with thinly sliced cucumber arranged over the top.

Crudites with aioli sauce

Ingredients   **Makes one bowl**
  2 egg yolks
  225 ml (8 fl oz) olive oil
  1 tablespoon lemon juice
  salt and black pepper
  5 large cloves garlic
  selection of raw vegetable pieces – celery, tomatoes, cucumber,
      radishes, red, green and yellow peppers, carrot sticks, fennel,
      cauliflower and apple slices

Method
Slice both ends off each garlic clove and place on a chopping board. Squash with the blade of a heavy knife and skin will peel off easily. Purée the garlic in a blender or mortar with salt to taste and little of the oil. Stir in the lemon juice.

In a separate bowl, beat the egg yolks until pale but not foamy, then add the remainder of the oil slowly, beating vigorously. Add garlic purée, pepper and more salt if desired.

Stand aside to allow flavour to mature. This is best made early in the day to serve in the evening.

Antipasto

When buying processed meats such as salami and garlic sausage, it is always best to buy pre-packed meats with a list of ingredients on the pack. Sadly, those made in the UK often have modified starch or other starches such as potato flour added. Most European-made varieties are starch-free.

On a large flat serving dish, arrange a selection of cold meats: salamis, various hams, garlic sausage, sliced smoked turkey breast, etc. Alternate with cheese cut into sticks or cubes, olives, strips of cucumber, red and green peppers, spring onions, anchovy fillets, prawns, tiny lettuce leaves and melon slices.

Marinaded mushrooms

Ingredients   **Makes one bowl**
250 g (8½ oz) button mushrooms
100 ml (4 fl oz) olive oil
3 tablespoons lemon juice
½ teaspoon garlic granules
¼ teaspoon salt
2 tablespoons chopped parsley
black pepper

Method
Wash the mushrooms and allow them to dry while preparing
the marinade. Combine the oil, lemon juice, garlic granules, salt
and pepper in a screw-top jar and shake well. Pour into a
serving dish and add the chopped parsley. Remove the stalks
from the mushrooms and slice thinly. Toss lightly in the
marinade and allow to stand at least 4 hours or overnight.

To serve, remove the mushrooms from the marinade with a
slotted spoon and place in a small serving dish. Delicious as an
addition to a green salad.

Fromage blanc and anchovy dip

Ingredients   **Makes one bowl**
500 g (1 lb) fromage blanc
8 anchovy fillets
2 level tablespoons capers
1 teaspoon mild French mustard with peppercorns
2 tablespoons chopped chives
1 tablespoon chopped parsley

Method
Thoroughly beat the fromage blanc until it is smooth. Drain the
anchovies (if they are packed in brine you should also rinse
them), remove as much of the backbone as possible, chop and
add to the fromage blanc with all the other ingredients,
reserving a few of the chopped chives.

Refrigerate for a few hours and serve in a small dish,
sprinkled with the remaining chives.

Onion dip

Ingredients   **Makes one bowl**

    1 small can Nestlé cream
    1 teaspoon vinegar
    1 teaspoon onion granules
    ¼ teaspoon salt

Method
Empty contents of the can into a small dish, add onion granules
and salt, then mix well. A dash of tomato ketchup or a teaspoon
of mild mustard can also be added, if desired.

Prosciutto and papaw

Looks and tastes exotic and tropical – actually it is very easy
and quick to prepare. Could also be used as a salad.

Ingredients   **Serves four**

    1 papaw
    ½ red pepper
    ½ green pepper
    4 tablespoons olive oil
    2 tablespoons dry white wine
    ½ clove garlic or ½ teaspoon garlic granules
    salt and pepper
    4 slices of prosciutto ham – most supermarket deli sections stock
        this thin, darkish Italian raw dried ham nowadays, but if
        you can't get it, substitute thin slices of any ham.

Method
Cut the papaw into quarters and remove the seeds. Place on a
serving dish and arrange a slice of ham over each quarter. Blend
the oil, white wine, salt and pepper and crushed garlic well, or
put all in a screw-top jar and shake. (Use your favourite
viniagrette dressing if you wish – just make sure it contains no
modified starch.)

Slice the peppers thinly, place in a separate bowl, pour the
dressing over and mix well. Place a spoonful of dressed peppers
on top of the ham on each papaw slice and refrigerate until
ready to serve.

Salmon pâté

Ingredients **Makes one bowl**
  220 g (8 oz) can red salmon
  125 g (4½ oz) pack cream cheese
  2 tablespoons lime or lemon juice
  black pepper
  1 tablespoon chopped chives
  100 ml (4 fl oz) any starch-free mayonnaise
  125 g (4½ oz) melted unsalted butter

Method
Beat the cream cheese until soft. Add the drained salmon, chopped chives, mayonnaise, juice, chives and pepper and blend well. Add the melted butter, then blend until smooth. Spoon into a serving dish and refrigerate until set.

Cucumber and chive mousse

Ingredients **Serves four**
  1 medium cucumber
  150 g (5 oz) cottage cheese
  85 ml (3 fl oz) Hellman's real mayonnaise (without modified
    starch)
  salt and pepper
  1 tablespoon finely chopped chives
  85 ml (3 fl oz) whipping cream
  ½ tablespoon (½ sachet) powdered gelatine
  4 tablespoons water
  1 rounded teaspoon fruit sugar or caster sugar
  chopped parsley

Method
Beat the cottage cheese with an electric beater or blend until smooth. Stir in the mayonnaise. Peel and quarter the cucumber lengthways, remove the seeds and chop finely. Chop the chives. Add these to the cottage cheese mixture.
  Put the water into a small saucepan, stir in the sugar and pepper. Sprinkle the gelatine over the top, stir and allow to stand for a few moments. Put the pan on a low heat and stir to dissolve. Remove and cool.

Stir the cottage cheese mixture into the gelatine. Beat the cream until stiff and fold into gelatine mixture. Spoon into small individual ramekin dishes which have been lightly rubbed round with paper towel dipped in cooking oil, and chill in the refrigerator until set.

To serve, run a knife around inside of ramekin to loosen the mousse, upturn onto lettuce leaves and garnish with chopped parsley.

Tuna mousse

Ingredients   **Serves four**
185 g (6 oz) can tuna in brine, drained
2 tablespoons starch-free mayonnaise
2 tablespoons lemon juice
1 small onion finely chopped
1 tablespoon chopped parsley
1 tablespoon tomato purée
½ teaspoon French Dijon mustard
½ teaspoon honey-mustard
3 teaspoons gelatine
2 tablespoons water

Method
Blend the first eight ingredients until smooth. Put the water in a small saucepan and sprinkle the gelatine over. Allow it to stand for a few minutes and then gently dissolve, stirring well, over a low heat or over a pan of simmering water. Stir into the tuna mixture.

Rinse four individual ramekins or one larger serving dish with cold water – do not allow to dry. Spoon the mixture into the dish(es) and refrigerate for several hours or overnight. To serve, run a knife around the inside of the ramekins to loosen mousse and upturn, or upturn larger dish wrapped in a tea towel dipped in hot water, until mousse slides out.

Veal and ham terrine

So many bought pâtés and terrines contain breadcrumbs or modified starch. This recipe is a wonderful starter but also an ideal luncheon dish with a salad.

Ingredients
500 g (1 lb) English farmhouse veal steak
250 g (10 oz) ham
500 g (1 lb) ham fat
250 g (10 oz) chicken livers
1 tablespoon brandy
3 bayleaves
1 tablespoon canned green peppercorns
1 teaspoon dried onion granules
1 teaspoon dried garlic granules
30 g (1 oz) salted butter
2 eggs
2 teaspoons dried herbes de Provence or mixed herbs
salt and pepper

Method
Marinate the chicken livers in the brandy for 30 minutes. Mince the veal, the ham and a quarter of the ham fat in a food processor or mincer in batches, until quite fine. Process the chicken livers with brandy until fine, or if using a mincer, drain, reserving brandy, and mince until fine. Add the livers and brandy to veal mixture.

Beat the eggs lightly and add to the meat mixture with the peppercorns, herbs, salt and black pepper to taste. Melt the butter, stir in the onion and garlic granules, remove from the heat, add to the meat mixture and blend well.

Arrange the bayleaves in the base of a narrow, oven-proof dish or loaf tin (20 cm × 10 cm or 8 × 4 inches). Slice the remaining ham fat thinly and completely line the tin, allowing enough fat to overlap so that it can be folded over to cover the top. Pile the meat mixture into the tin and press down firmly, covering the top with overlapping fat. Cover with foil and place the whole container in a *baine marie* (baking dish with hot water halfway up its sides) and bake in a moderate oven (180°C/350°F or gas mark 4) for $1\frac{1}{2}$ hours.

Remove from the water, cool slightly and place a chopping board on top of the terrine, weighing it down with something heavy. When cold, refrigerate until required. Delicious served cold with bitter orange sauce (see page 197).

Simple scallops

Two easy recipes suitable as a starter for three, or main course for two.

Version 1 ingredients
12 scallops
50 g (2 oz) unsalted butter
garlic granules

Method
Sprinkle the scallops lightly with the garlic granules. Melt the butter in a heavy frying pan and when it begins to foam, add the scallops and cook for about 3–4 minutes each side. Serve with the hot garlicky pan juices poured over.

A richer sauce can be made (after removing the scallops to a warm plate) by blending a dash of dry white wine with the pan drippings and adding a tablespoon or so of double cream. Stir well and when it begins to bubble, pour over scallops.

Version 2 ingredients
12 scallops
juice 1 lime
4 tablespoons chopped fresh coriander leaves
50–75 g (2–3 oz) unsalted butter

Method
Melt the butter in a frying pan over a low heat, add the lime juice and coriander leaves and blend well. Turn up the heat and add the scallops. Cook for 3–4 minutes on each side, then serve with the pan juices poured over.

Show-off scallops

Ingredients   **Serves two or three**
12 or so scallops – depending on their size
garlic granules
50 g (2 oz) unsalted butter
100 ml (4 fl oz) brandy – apple or apricot brandy is good
150 ml ($\frac{1}{4}$ pint) double cream
1 tablespoon chopped chives

Method
Sprinkle the scallops with the garlic granules. Melt the butter in a frying pan or chafing dish, add the scallops and cook over high heat for 3 minutes on one side. Meanwhile, heat the brandy in a small saucepan. Remove the scallops from the heat, pour the brandy over the scallops, light the brandy with a match and, when it burns out, return the pan to a high heat and cook for 2 minutes. Add the cream, stir until hot again. Pour into serving dishes, then sprinkle with chopped chives.

Easy chicken liver pâté

Ingredients   **Serves four**
500 g (1 lb) chicken livers
85 ml (3 fl oz) brandy
90 g ($3\frac{1}{2}$ oz) butter
1 teaspoon onion granules
1 teaspoon garlic granules
85 ml (3 fl oz) double cream
salt and pepper
$\frac{1}{2}$ teaspoon dried mixed herbs

Method
Trim the livers and cut in half. Marinate in the brandy for at least 2 hours. Strain, reserving the liquid.

Melt half the butter in a pan, add the livers and cook for 3 minutes over a moderate heat. Add the brandy liquid and cook for a further minute. Remove from the heat, purée the liver in a blender or food processor. Melt the remaining butter, add the onion, garlic granules and mixed herbs, then add to the liver mixture and mix thoroughly. Add the cream and seasoning to taste. Place in a serving dish and refrigerate overnight.

Caviar pie

Ingredients   **Serves eight to ten as an entrée**
8 large hard-boiled eggs
80 g (3 oz) unsalted butter, melted
180 ml (6 fl oz) thick sour cream
100 ml (4 fl oz) Hellman's real or any starch-free mayonnaise
1 teaspoon onion granules
1 teaspoon sharp Dijon mustard
100 ml (4 oz) jar caviar

Method
Finely chop the eggs and combine with the melted butter, mayonnaise, onion granules, mustard and 60 ml (2 fl oz) of the sour cream. Spread the mixture onto a quiche or pie plate. Spread the remaining 100 ml (4 fl oz) of sour cream over the top and chill overnight.

Before serving, spread the caviar evenly over the sour cream. Cut into slices and serve on lettuce leaves with lemon wedges.

Fresh goat's cheese with herbs

Ingredients   **Serves two to three**
500 g (1 lb) fresh goat's cheese
2 small spring onions
1 wine glass full of dry white wine
3 tablespoons olive oil
2–3 tablespoons any or all of these herbs, finely chopped –
    parsley, chives, basil, chervil, tarragon, coriander

Method
Remove and discard the cheese skin or rind. Ideally, the cheese should be quite soft, but if it is more mature with a pungent aroma, add a little milk or single cream, blending it in with a fork until the texture is that of a fresh cheese. Add the olive oil and wine, then the finely chopped onions and herbs. Put in an airtight container and refrigerate for a few hours before serving. This recipe can be made a couple of days before use.

Smoked salmon curls

Ingredients   **Serves two to three**
  225 g (8½ oz) smoked salmon
  4 tablespoons double cream
  225 g (8½ oz) soft cream cheese with herbs
  50 g (2 oz) unsalted butter, softened
  1 tablespoon chopped chives
  freshly ground black pepper (optional)

Method
Separate the thin slices of smoked salmon and spread them out
on a layer of foil. Combine the remaining ingredients into a
spreadable consistency and spread over the salmon. Roll up the
salmon like a Swiss roll and wrap in the foil. Chill for 2 hours.
Unroll and with a sharp knife, slice and serve.

Tomato and mozzarella salad

Ingredients   **Serves six**
  5 beef tomatoes
  5 buffalo Mozzarella cheeses
  2 tins anchovy fillets
  fresh basil
  mild black Spanish olives in brine, pitted
  extra virgin olive oil
  freshly ground black pepper

Method
Slice the tomatoes and Mozzarella thinly. Arrange on a large
serving plate, overlapping the alternating tomato and cheese
slices. Scatter the olives around the tomatoes, then drain the
anchovy fillets and arrange on top.
  Tear off small basil leaves and arrange on top, or roughly
chop larger basil leaves (they tend to discolour slightly when
chopped). Drizzle with olive oil, sprinkle with pepper and
serve.

Gravadlax

So simple to make and about quarter the price of the commercial product. Trout fillets make a very good substitute but you can also use any white-fleshed fish.

Ingredients   **Serves four to six**
1 whole side (fillet) of a smallish salmon or ½ salmon
4 tablespoons soft brown or raw sugar
4 tablespoons rock salt
1 tablespoon crushed white peppercorns
about 3 generous bunches of dill

Method
Crush the peppercorns with a pestle and mortar or grind in a pepper grinder – not too finely. Combine with the sugar and salt in a small bowl. Lay half the dill on a piece of foil, generous enough to wrap well around the fillet, then sprinkle with half the salt and sugar, layering it thickly. Place the salmon fillet on top, skin side down. Check the flesh side along the backbone, removing any bones. Sprinkle with the remaining salt and sugar mixture, then lay the remaining dill on top. Wrap fillet tightly in foil, making sure it is lying flat. Place on a plate and place another plate on top. Put in refrigerator and weigh the plate down with several cans of beer or similar.

Leave pressed down for 24 hours. Turn upside-down still pressed between the plates and weigh again for a further 24 hours.

Remove from the refrigerator, peel off foil. The salmon is now cured and ready to eat. Serve with sour cream and extra dill.

Fish

Smoked haddock with cream

Ingredients   **Serves two**
  350 g (12 oz) smoked haddock
  175 ml (8 fl oz) double cream
  freshly ground black pepper
  butter
  freshly grated Parmesan cheese or, if preferred, 2–3 oz of a mild
     cheese such as Emmental or Jarslburg

Method
Bring just enough water to cover the fish to boil, then turn the
heat down. Add the fish and gently poach for about 5 minutes.
Drain, remove the skin, and flake the fish removing any bones.

Butter an oven-proof dish, add the fish and pour over the
cream. Season with pepper and sprinkle with grated cheese.
Freshly grated Parmesan would be my choice but you can use
the packaged, pre-grated kind – or either of the other cheeses
mentioned above. Bake in a pre-heated oven at 200°C (400°F or
gas mark 6) for 20 minutes or until bubbling.

Mustard and honeyed fish

Ingredients   **Serves two**
  8 small fish fillets
  2 tablespoons grated Parmesan cheese
  2 teaspoons olive oil
  1 tablespoon lemon juice
  2 teaspoons French mustard
  1 teaspoon honey
  150 ml ($\frac{1}{4}$ pint) water

Method
Make the sauce first. Combine the oil, lemon juice, mustard and
honey in a small saucepan. Stir in the water and simmer
constantly over a low heat allowing the sauce to thicken.

Place the fish on a griller tray, sprinkle with half the cheese.
Grill for 3 minutes and turn over, sprinkle with the remaining
cheese, then grill for a further 3 minutes. Serve with the sauce.

Fish with lime sauce

Ingredients   **Serves two**

14 medium-sized fish fillets of your choice – cod, coley, halibut,
    mullet are all suitable
75 ml (2½ fl oz) fresh lime juice
4 tablespoons white wine vinegar
1 teaspoon garlic granules
1 tablespoon fruit sugar or honey
2 tablespoons cracked black peppercorns
30 g (1 oz) butter, preferably unsalted
100 ml (4 fl oz) water
100 ml 100 g (4 oz) butter extra

Method

Arrange the fish in a shallow dish in a single layer. Combine
the lime juice, vinegar, sugar (honey) and garlic and pour over
the fish. Cover and refrigerate for 2 hours. Remove the fish
from the marinade, strain and reserve the liquid. Remove the
fish and drain. Sprinkle both sides with peppercorns.

Heat 30 g (1 oz) butter in a frying pan, add the fish in a single
layer and cook for about 4 minutes on each side or until cooked
when tested with a fork. Remove the fish, place it in a serving
dish and keep warm.

Heat the marinade in a small saucepan, add the water and
bring to the boil. Reduce the heat and simmer uncovered until
the mixture is reduced by about half. Chop the extra butter into
small pieces and add slowly, whisking continuously until the
sauce is thickish and smooth. Serve over the fish.

Danish fish with blue cheese

Ingredients   **Serves two**

2 slices fresh halibut
125 g (4½ oz) butter
salt
60 g (2 oz) Danish blue cheese
1 tablespoon lemon juice
2 wedges lemon
chopped parsley

Method

Wash the fish and blot dry. Lightly sprinkle with salt and scatter several small pieces of butter on a flame-proof dish on which the fish is to be grilled and served.

Meanwhile melt the remaining butter, blue cheese and lemon juice together in a separate saucepan. Start to grill fish, basting with the cheese mixture. Continue cooking until the fish flakes when pricked with a fork or after about 7 minutes.

Serve sprinkled with parsley and decorated with lemon wedges.

Salmon with vermouth sauce

Ingredients   **Serves four**

    4 *medium salmon cutlets*
    675 ml (24 fl oz) water
    75 ml (2½ fl oz) lemon juice
    225 ml (8 fl oz) double cream
    4 tablespoons dry vermouth
    2 further teaspoons lemon juice
    ½ teaspoon garlic granules
    1 tablespoon drained capers
    1 teaspoon chopped fresh thyme
    2 tablespoons chopped fresh basil
    1 teaspoon chopped fresh coriander
    1 tablespoon chopped chives

Method

Begin to make the sauce first. Chop all the fresh herbs ready to add to the sauce. Combine the cream and vermouth in a small saucepan and gently bring to the boil. Reduce the heat and simmer gently for about 10 minutes.

Meanwhile, combine the water and lemon juice in a large frying pan and bring to the boil, reduce the heat and poach the salmon for about 7 minutes or until just tender. Remove to a serving dish and keep hot. Add 2 further teaspoons lemon juice and the fresh herbs to sauce just before serving and stir to blend. Serve over cooked fish.

Smoked fish puff

This dish is very low in calories.

Ingredients   **Serves two**
  150 g (6 oz) smoked haddock or other white smoked fish
  2 teaspoons Heinz tomato sauce (or any starch-free ketchup)
  2 medium eggs, separated
  pepper
  butter

Method
Flake the haddock, mix with the tomato sauce and egg yolks. Season with pepper. Whisk the egg whites until stiff and fold into the fish mixture. Place in a small buttered oven-proof dish and cook for 15–20 minutes at a medium heat 180°C (350°F or gas mark 4). Serve with salad.

Smoked salmon omelette

This sounds expensive but it can be made quite cheaply from smoked salmon offcuts, often available from delis and supermarkets. Check to make sure they're a fresh, orangey-pink colour and moist, not hard and shiny.

Ingredients   **Serves one**
  50 g (2 oz) butter
  2 large eggs
  pinch salt
  freshly ground black pepper
  4 tablespoons shredded smoked salmon trimmings
  1 tablespoon chopped parsley

Method
Whisk the eggs and salt with a fork until just blended. Melt half the butter in a small, heavy frying pan over a medium heat and put in the egg mixture. Reduce the heat and stir with a wooden spoon, making sure the eggs do not stick. Before the mixture cooks completely, take the pan off the heat, add the second piece of butter and smoked salmon, stir to blend and serve with chopped parsley.

Fish fillets with apricot sauce

Ingredients   **Serves six**
  6 large white fish fillets
  425 g can or pack of apricot nectar or juice, or purée a can of
    apricot pieces
  2 teaspoons onion granules
  2 teaspoons Greek yoghurt
  1 tablespoon fresh mint

Method
Place the fish in a lightly buttered baking dish. Combine the
remaining ingredients and pour over the fish. Cover with a lid
or foil. Bake in a moderate oven at 180°C (350°F or gas mark 4)
for about 45 minutes or until the fish is tender.

Slimmer's seafood salad

Ingredients   **Serves two**
  350 g (12 oz) white fish fillet
  1 tablespoon lemon juice
  ½ teaspoon salt
  freshly ground black pepper
  1 large beefsteak tomato
  100 g (4 oz) cucumber
  2 tablespoons chopped chives
  2 teaspoons capers
  4–5 anchovy fillets
  3 tablespoons natural low-fat yoghurt
  1 tablespoon starch-free mayonnaise
  1 teaspoon starch-free tomato ketchup
  100 g (4 oz) peeled prawns
  lettuce leaves for serving

Method
Wash and skin the fish and cut into cubes. Place in a single layer
over the bottom of a wide saucepan or frying pan. Pour over
enough water just to cover the fish. Add the lemon juice, salt
and pepper, and heat until the water is simmering. Poach
gently for 10–15 minutes, or until cooked. Drain and allow to
cool.

Dice the tomato and cucumber and mix with capers and chopped chives. Dice the anchovy fillets and mix with the mayonnaise, yoghurt and tomato ketchup. Toss the fish cubes into the salad vegetables, then add freshly ground black pepper. Line a serving plate with lettuce leaves. Pile the fish mixture onto the leaves, then pour the dressing over. Scatter prawns on top and serve.

Crusty fish cutlets

Ingredients   **Serves four**
   4 *large white fish cutlets*
   2 *tablespoons lemon juice*
   1 *tablespoon dry white wine*
   75 g (3 oz) *ground (blanched) almonds*
   125 g (4 oz) *grated mild cheese*
   2 *teaspoons Dijon peppercorn mustard*
   2 *tablespoons chopped fresh parsley*
   1 *tablespoon chopped fresh chives*
   1 *tablespoon chopped fresh dill*
   1 *teaspoon garlic granules*
   60 g (2 oz) *melted butter*

Method
Place the fish cutlets in single layer in a lightly greased oven-proof dish, sprinkle with the lemon juice and wine. In a small bowl, combine the remaining ingredients and spoon evenly over the fish. Bake uncovered in a moderate oven at 180°C (350°F or gas mark 4) for about 40 minutes or until the fish is tender when tested with a fork.

Baked fish with herb butter pockets

Ingredients   **Serves six**
  6 small whole fish or portions of a large whole fish
  250 g (10 oz) salted butter
  4 bacon rashers
  4 tablespoons chopped fresh parsley
  1 tablespoon chopped fresh chives
  1 tablespoon chopped fresh thyme
  4 tablespoons Parmesan cheese
  1 teaspoon garlic granules
  ½ teaspoon onion granules
  1 tablespoon lemon juice

Method
The fish should be boned but left as whole as possible. Dice the
bacon. Beat the butter in a small bowl until creamy, then add
the bacon, herbs, cheese, garlic, onion and lemon juice. Blend
well. Spread the mixture on the inside of the fish and wrap each
serving in foil.

Bake in an oven-proof dish in a moderate oven at 180°C
(350°F or gas mark 4) for about 30 minutes or so, depending on
the size of the fish (peel back the foil and test with a fork for
tenderness). Serve with lemon wedges. This can also be cooked
on a barbecue.

Salmon pizza-ish

Ingredients   **Serves two**
  213 g (8 oz) can pink salmon
  2 tablespoons double cream
  several tomatoes – the sweeter the better, any size will do
  1–2 teaspoons garlic granules
  freshly ground black pepper
  1–2 teaspoons dried mixed herbs or Italian herbs
  ½–1 cup grated mild Cheddar
  ½ dozen pitted black olives and/or strips of salami

Method
Drain the salmon and turn into a small gratin dish. Press it
evenly over the bottom. Dribble double cream all over the

salmon. Slice the tomatoes and arrange in a layer over the salmon. Sprinkle with a little freshly ground black pepper and then with the garlic granules. Grate the cheese and spread over the tomatoes. Sprinkle with dried herbs. Slice the olives and/or salami and arrange over the cheese. Cook in a hot oven at 220°C (425°F or gas mark 7) until it looks like a cooked pizza.

Creamy salmon bake

Ingredients   **Serves two**

1 medium 213 g (8 oz) can and 1 small 105 g
   (4 oz) can pink salmon
4 rashers bacon
325 ml (12 fl oz) whipping cream
3 eggs
salt and pepper to taste
1 tablespoon grated Parmesan cheese
2 tablespoons chopped parsley

Method
Dice the bacon and fry gently until crisp. Drain the salmon reserving the liquid, flake, remove the bones and spread evenly on the bottom of a medium-sized oven-proof dish.

Beat the cream until thick. In a separate bowl beat the eggs until thick and creamy. Fold the cheese, salmon liquid and parsley into the egg mixture and blend well. Fold in the cream and add salt and pepper if desired (take care – canned salmon can be very salty).

Sprinkle the diced bacon over the salmon. Pour the egg mixture over the top. Bake in a moderately hot oven at 190°C (375F or gas mark 5) for 10 minutes. Reduce the heat to moderately low 170°C (325°F or gas mark 3) and bake for a further 30–35 minutes, or until the bake is set and beginning to brown on top.

Main courses
Lemon-garlic chicken strips in cream sauce

You can serve the chicken without the sauce if you're trying to cut down on calories.

Ingredients   **Serves two**

3 boneless chicken breasts
lemon juice
2 teaspoons garlic granules
freshly ground black pepper
30 g (1 oz) butter
olive oil for frying
2 tablespoons crème fraîche or Greek yoghurt
½ teaspoon fruit sugar
100 ml (4 fl oz) white wine or water
salt to taste
handful chopped parsley

Method
Remove any gristle or fat from the chicken breasts and slice each breast into four or five thinnish strips. Place on a plate and squeeze the lemon juice over, turning and making sure both sides are coated in juice. Sprinkle one side liberally with garlic granules and lightly with pepper.

Heat the olive oil and butter in frying pan over a high heat. Drop the chicken, garlic-side down, into oil and butter and fry quickly for about 3 minutes. Just before turning sprinkle with the remaining garlic and pepper. Turn and fry for about 3–5 minutes depending on thickness (test with a fork to make sure the chicken is just cooked – do not overcook.)

Remove from heat and place the chicken in a serving dish. Keep warm. Pour excess oil and butter from the pan and replace on a low heat. Add the fruit sugar and wine, stir until dissolved and all the brownings from the pan are scraped off. Add salt to taste. Cook for a few minutes until mixture thickens slightly. Add crème fraîche or Greek yoghurt and stir well until the sauce reaches the desired thickness. More wine or water can be added if necessary.

Pour the sauce over the chicken strips. Add the parsley and serve.

Chicken marsala

Ingredients   **Serves four**
  4 skinless chicken breasts
  30 g (1 oz) butter
  olive oil
  1–2 teaspoons garlic granules
  4 anchovy fillets
  12 capers
  4 slices Mozzarella cheese
  1 tablespoon chopped parsley
  3 tablespoons marsala wine
  150 ml (¼ pint) cream
  salt and pepper

Method
Remove any gristle or fat from the chicken breasts and sprinkle
with garlic granules. Melt the butter in a pan with enough olive
oil for frying, then add the chicken breasts and cook for a few
minutes on each side until lightly browned and almost cooked
through. Remove the pan from the heat.

Lay a slice of cheese over each breast and top each with an
anchovy fillet, three capers and a sprinkle of parsley. Return
the pan to moderate heat and cook a further 5 minutes. Remove
from the pan and place the chicken in a serving dish. Keep
warm.

Add marsala to the pan drippings and return to the heat.
Scrape the pan brownings off the bottom, reduce the heat, add
the cream and simmer gently for a few minutes until sauce
thickens. Season to taste with salt and pepper.

Pour over the chicken breasts and serve.

Roast chicken with lemon and herb sauce

This simple way to roast chicken is my family's favourite. I've
discovered that the large family size bird is usually the most
tender, so I often cut one in half, right down the centre, and
then cook one half (which serves three) and freeze the other.
The chicken must be roasted alone. Roast vegetables in a
separate dish, using the herby chicken/butter fat from a
previous roasting.

Ingredients   **Serves three to six**

any size chicken
$\frac{1}{2}$ *a lemon*
garlic granules
75 g (3 oz) butter
2 fresh bayleaves and 2 sprigs fresh rosemary or sprinkle dried herbs

Sauce (optional)

1–2 teaspoons honey-mustard
slosh white wine or water
2 tablespoons Greek yoghurt or crème fraîche
salt

Method

Untruss the chicken and place in a roasting or oven-proof dish. Squeeze the half lemon over the chicken, then place the lemon in the cavity inside the chicken. Sprinkle the chicken with garlic granules. Press thin slices of butter all over the chicken breast and legs. Push the fresh herbs into the cavity so that they are just sticking out, or press them over the top of chicken (or sprinkle the chicken with dried herbs).

Cover with foil or a roasting bag and place in a moderate oven at 180°C (350°F or gas mark 4) for $1\frac{1}{2}$ hours. Remove from oven and check for 'doneness' (if the juices run clear when prodded with a fork, it is cooked). If it is not cooked enough, return to the oven with the foil removed to allow browning.

When cooked, remove the chicken from oven, place it on an oven-proof dish and stand in warm place. Skim the fat from the roasting dish by standing it on a tilt and allowing the thick chicken stock to settle to the bottom. With a large, flat spoon, gently skim off the clear fat, reserving it in a clean jam jar. When you have skimmed off as much fat as you can, place the roasting dish with the remaining chicken stock on a very low heat. Stir in the honey-mustard, scraping any brownings from the edge of the pan. Add the wine or water and stir, tasting and adding salt as desired. Add the yoghurt and stir to blend, until the sauce begins to thicken. Serve the sauce as gravy.

If you don't want to make the sauce, reserve the remaining chicken stock in a jar or freeze in ice cube containers.

Chicken kebabs

You need to soak the kebab skewers in water for about an hour before cooking, to prevent burning.

Ingredients   **Serves two to three**
   3 skinless chicken breasts
   2 tablespoons no-starch vinaigrette or French dressing
   1 tablespoon orange juice
   1 tablespoon lemon juice
   1 tablespoon water
   2 tablespoons grated Parmesan cheese
   2 tablespoons chopped fresh basil
   2 tablespoons chopped fresh parsley
   2 tablespoons chopped chives

Method
Remove any gristle or fat from the chicken and chop into $2\frac{1}{2}$ cm (1 inch) chunks. Combine all the other ingredients in a bowl, add chicken and marinate, refrigerated, for at least an hour. Remove the chicken, reserving the marinade. Thread the chicken onto skewers and grill on both sides under high heat, basting frequently with marinade, until cooked.

Orange-minty chicken

Ingredients   **Serves four**
   4 large skinless chicken breasts
   4 tablespoons chopped fresh mint
   100 ml (4 fl oz) white vinegar
   225 ml (8 fl oz) orange juice
   1 tablespoon fruit sugar
   50 g (2 oz) butter

Method
Flatten the chicken breasts with a meat mallet or a rolling pin until thin. Scatter the mint evenly over each fillet and roll up tightly, securing with a cocktail stick. Bake covered in an oven-proof dish in moderate oven at 180°C (350°F or gas mark 4) for about 25 minutes or until the chicken is tender.
   Meanwhile make the sauce. Combine the vinegar and sugar

in small saucepan, stirring over a low heat until the sugar is
dissolved. Bring it to the boil, then boil rapidly without stirring
until the mixture turns a light golden brown. Add the orange
juice and bring to the boil again. Reduce the heat and simmer
until reduced by about half. Add butter and stir until blended.

Remove the cooked chicken from the oven, remove the
cocktail sticks and slice into rounds. Serve with sauce.

Cheese stuffed chicken breasts

Ingredients   **Serves four**
   4 large skinless chicken breasts
   125 g (4 oz) cottage cheese
   2 tablespoons chopped chives
   ¼ teaspoon dried tarragon leaves
   1 tablespoon (approximately) jellied chicken stock
      (see 'Handy Hints' on page 218)
   225 ml (8 fl oz) water

Sauce
   100 ml (4 fl oz) water or stock
   2 tablespoons lemon juice
   2 teaspoons fruit sugar
   30 g (1 oz) butter
   1 tablespoon plain yoghurt

Method
Remove any gristle or fat from the chicken breasts and cut a
pocket in the thickest part. Press the cottage cheese through a
sieve and combine with the chives and tarragon. Stuff pockets
with this mixture. Place the breasts in an oven-proof dish.
Combine the stock and water, pour over the chicken and bake,
covered, for about 20 minutes in a moderate oven at 180°C
(350°F or gas mark 4). Remove from the heat, place the chicken
on a serving plate and keep warm.

Measure the remaining liquid and make it up to 100 ml (4 fl
oz) with additional water if necessary. Add the lemon juice,
sugar, butter and yoghurt. Blend over a medium heat just until
it thickens. Serve over the chicken.

Cary's rich cream & brandy chicken casserole

Ingredients   **Serves three to four**
  1 large pre-cooked chicken or 6 pre-cooked breasts (cold)
  soft dried apricots
  450 ml (16 fl oz) fresh orange juice and grated zest of
    1 large orange
  segments of 1 large orange
  sprinkle of mixed Italian herbs
  freshly ground black pepper
  100 ml (4 fl oz) double cream
  225 ml (8 fl oz) white wine
  4 tablespoons brandy

Method
Pull whole chicken into serving size pieces or arrange breasts
in ovenproof dish. Wash and zest the orange (taking care only
to get the orange zest, not any of the pale, bitter pith) then peel
and divide the segments. Combine the orange juice, zest,
apricots and orange segments. Pour all over chicken. Sprinkle
with mixed herbs and cook, covered in a moderate oven 180°C
(350°F or Gas mark 4) for 20–30 minutes or until completely
warmed through. Blend the cream with the wine. Remove the
chicken from the heat and pour cream and wine over, blending
with the juices and basting the chicken well. Turn up the heat
and cook in hot oven at 200°C (400°F or Gas mark 6) for further
10 minutes. Remove from the heat and add the brandy (a good
slosh). Blend into the sauce and serve.

Slimmers' simple chicken

So easy and delicious. I usually make twice as much as I need
and slice or cube the cold chicken into a salad the next day.

Ingredients
  chicken breasts – 1 or 2 for each person
  1 lemon
  freshly ground black pepper
  garlic granules (optional)

Method
Remove any skin and gristle or fat from the chicken. Sprinkle lemon juice lightly over both sides of each breast. Place each breast on a piece of foil and sprinkle with garlic granules (if desired) and black pepper. Fold the foil around each breast and place in an oven-proof dish. Cook for 20–25 minutes in a hot oven at 190°C (375°F or gas mark 5). Don't overcook – open one parcel and check for 'doneness' at 20 minutes. If you plan to use any of the chicken cold, leave it in the foil until the next day as it improves the flavour.

Breast of chicken in rum crumbs

Ingredients   **Serves two**
  2 *large skinless chicken breasts*
  4 *tablespoons ground almonds*
  5 *tablespoons rum*
  1 *tablespoon strawberry or blackberry or black cherry jelly (jam jelly)*
  1 *teaspoon honey-mustard*
  50 *g (2 oz) butter*
  olive oil for frying

Method
Flatten each chicken breast with a rolling pin, meat mallet or the edge of a saucer until thin. Place the ground almonds on a plate. Pour 4 tablespoons of rum into a shallow dish, dip the chicken breasts in it and then dip them in the ground almonds.

Over a medium heat, melt the butter, add the olive oil and sauté each chicken slice for a few minutes each side, or until golden. Meanwhile, combine the jelly, honey-mustard and a tablespoon of rum over a low heat. Place the chicken on a serving dish, pour the sauce over and serve.

Roast chicken with mustard

Ingredients   **Serves four**
    4 large chicken pieces including bone and skin
    4 level tablespoons Dijon mustard with peppercorns
    4 sprigs of fresh herbs – such as rosemary or sage or lemon balm
    8 rashers of bacon

Method
Arrange the chicken pieces in an oven-proof dish, spread mustard over each, add a sprig of fresh herbs and cover each with two rashers of bacon. Bake in a hot oven at 220°C (425°F or gas mark 7) for 25 minutes. May also be grilled or barbecued.

French roast chicken

Ingredients   **Serves four to six**
    family-sized roasting chicken
    approximately 90 g (3½ oz) salted butter
    2 tablespoons chopped parsley
    1 teaspoon chopped tarragon
    1 teaspoon Dijon mustard
    2 fresh bayleaves
    2 sprigs fresh rosemary
    225 ml (8 fl oz) water
    100 ml (4 fl oz) white wine
    1–2 tablespoons chicken stock (see 'Handy Hints' on page 218)

Method
Beat the butter until soft. Add the parsley, tarragon and mustard and blend well. With your fingers, gently ease the skin away from chicken breast. Spread the butter mixture over the meat underneath the skin, covering as much of the breast as you can. Pull the skin back to cover the meat completely.

  Put the chicken on a baking dish. Stuff the bayleaves and rosemary into the chicken cavity. Blend the water, wine and chicken stock, then pour it over the chicken and cook uncovered, basting frequently, in a moderate oven at 180°C (350°F or gas mark 4) for about 1½ hours or until the juices run clear when the chicken is pierced with a fork. Make a gravy from the pan juices (see 'No-Starch Gravy' on page 194).

Chicken apple casserole

Ingredients   **Serves four**

    medium-sized chicken
    50 g (2 oz) butter
    2 teaspoons garlic granules
    2 sweet apples
    2 teaspoons honey-mustard
    ½ pint apple juice
    1 teaspoon vinegar
    1 tablespoon plain mild yoghurt
    salt and pepper
    1 tablespoon double cream
    handful chopped parsley

Method

Untruss the chicken and sprinkle with garlic granules. Melt the butter in a frying pan and brown the chicken gently on both sides. Remove the pan from the heat. Place the chicken in a deep casserole dish (preferably with a lid) which is not too much larger than the bird, so that the juices can nearly cover it while cooking.

Peel and slice the apples into thick chunks. Return the pan to the heat and fry the apple chunks gently in the pan brownings. Remove from the heat and add the apple chunks to the casserole dish with the chicken. Return the pan to a low heat.

Stir in the honey-mustard, apple juice, vinegar and yoghurt, blending well with the brownings from the pan. Add salt and pepper to taste. Pour over chicken, cover and cook 1½–2 hours in a moderate oven at 180°C (350°F or gas mark 4), basting several times. When done, the chicken juices will run clear when the meat is pierced.

Remove the chicken to a serving plate and keep warm. Pour the sauce including the apple chunks into a small pan over a low heat. With a potato masher, mash the apple chunks as finely as possible – you can do this in a blender, but I rather like the sightly chunky texture of the masher method. Increase the heat and boil until reduced. Add a tablespoon of double cream (more if you wish) and boil until thick. Check the seasonings. Throw in a handful of chopped parsley and serve over the chicken.

Elizabeth David's poached chicken

Ingredients
Serves four to six

1 medium to large chicken
50 g (2 oz) butter
2 egg yolks
225 ml (8 fl oz) cream
bunch tarragon
lemon
salt and pepper

Method
Cut the lemon in half and rub the outside of the chicken with the juice. Chop the tarragon. Blend the butter with 1 tablespoon of the tarragon, add salt and pepper to taste and put inside the chicken. Place the chicken in a large saucepan and pour over enough water to barely cover it. Poach the chicken gently, uncovered, basting frequently with the liquid, until it is cooked. Leave it to cool in the stock. When cooled, remove the chicken to a deep serving dish.

Strain the stock. Beat the yolks of the eggs with the cream and another tablespoon of chopped tarragon. Heat about ½ pint of the stock in a small pan, pour a spoonful or two onto the egg and cream mixture, then pour it all back into the pan, stirring continuously until the sauce thickens, but do not make it too thick as it will continue to solidify as it cools.

Pour this over the chicken in the dish and leave it to get cold. Serve decorated with whole tarragon leaves.

Baked orange chicken

Ingredients
Serves four

4 chicken portions on the bone
50 g (2 oz) butter
225 ml (8 fl oz) orange juice
1 dessertspoon dried onion flakes
1 tablespoon homemade chicken stock (see page 218)
100 ml (4 fl oz) water
1 teaspoon dried tarragon
salt and pepper

Method
Skin the chicken pieces. Melt the butter in a frying pan and brown the chicken lightly on both sides. Remove from the heat and place the chicken in a casserole dish. Return the pan to the heat, add chicken stock, orange juice, water, onion flakes and tarragon. Stir to blend. Bring to the boil and remove immediately. Pour the sauce over the chicken, cover and cook in moderate oven at 180°C (350°F or gas mark 4) for 1 hour or until the chicken is tender.

Honey pepper chicken

You can make this dish from ready-cut individual pieces, but it is vey much cheaper to buy a large family-sized chicken and cut it up yourself.

Ingredients   **Serves four to eight**
  1 large-sized chicken
  225 ml (8 fl oz) honey
  juice 1 orange
  few drops lemon juice
  1 tablespoon pink or mixed peppercorns
  2 teaspoons wholegrain French mustard
  salt

Method
Cut the chicken in half and then into eight pieces, leaving the skin on. Place in a single layer in a large oven-proof dish.

Mix all the remaining ingredients together, season to taste and pour over the chicken. Dot with small nobs of butter (optional) and bake uncovered in a moderate to hot oven at 190°C (375°F or gas mark 5) for about an hour or until chicken juices run clear when the meat is pierced with a fork. Baste several times during cooking.

To serve, remove the pieces to a hot plate, skim the fat from the pan drippings and pour the remaining honey sauce into sauce boat. Serve with the chicken.

Rabbit with prunes

Ingredients   **Serves two to three**
  1 rabbit
  500 g (1 lb) soft pitted prunes
  1 bottle red wine
  2 tablespoons olive oil
  salt
  1 tablespoon dried onion pieces
  2 teaspoons garlic granules
  1 teaspoon whole pink or black or mixed peppercorns
  6 rashers smoked streaky bacon
  1 bouquet garni – fresh if possible

Method
Cover the prunes with the wine and soak for at least 2 hours beforehand. Cut the rabbit into serving size pieces, then brown them in the oil in a frying pan. Remove the pan from the heat and place the rabbit in a casserole dish.

Cut the bacon into small pieces, return the pan to the heat and brown the bacon in oil. Add the peppercorns, dried onion and garlic to the pan and cook over a low heat for a few seconds only, then pour the wine from the prunes into the pan and stir to blend the pan brownings with the liquid. Turn the heat up and leave to reduce (de-glaze) cooking juices until they thicken.

Pour the prunes into the casserole, place the bouquet garni on top and pour the pan juices over all. Cover and cook in a moderate oven (180°C, 350°F, gas mark 4) for at least 2 hours. This dish can be cooked at a lower heat if necessary – just allow extra time. It is even better cooked the day before and reheated.

Turkey schnitzel

Ingredients
  1 turkey breast for each person
  1 lemon
  garlic granules
  1 egg beaten with a little water
  ground almonds
  oil for cooking

Method
Place each turkey breast between cling-wrap or waxed paper and flatten with a heavy object such as a rolling pin or the back of a heavy frying pan.

Beat the egg with the water in a wide-based dish. Pour the ground almonds onto wax paper or a separate plate. Lay the turkey breasts on another plate and squeeze lemon juice over them. Turn and coat both sides. Sprinkle both sides with garlic granules. Dip each breast into the egg mixture and then into the ground almonds. Heat the oil in a heavy-based frying pan, and fry each schnitzel over a moderate heat until golden brown and completely cooked through. Serve with a slice of lemon.

Roast turkey with stuffing

Turkey is now available in so many sizes and prices, not to mention varieties, that it doesn't have to be kept for special occasions. This recipe is for a small, low-priced turkey, the sort you might have for a change for Sunday lunch or a dinner party. It cost me less than a roast of beef or leg of lamb or even pork. The long slow cooking is guaranteed to give you a moist, succulent result. The stuffing recipe is the same as I use at Christmas, but the amounts given are for a small turkey. Just double the ingredients for a large, Christmas-sized bird.

Ingredients   **Serves four to six**
fresh standard grade supermarket turkey about 6½ lb (the one I cooked was 6 lb 7½ oz or approximately 3.5 kg)
150 g (6 oz) stoned soft eating prunes
250 g (9 oz) soft dried apricots
300 g (about 3 medium-sized) eating apples
3 tablespoons dried mixed herbs – any sort
1 teaspoon garlic Italian seasoning (optional)
¼ teaspoon onion salt
¼ teaspoon onion granules
1 teaspoon garlic granules
sprinkle of salt and freshly ground black pepper
2 eggs
about 1 tablespoon garlic granules extra
125–175 g (4½–6½ oz) butter
4 sprigs of fresh rosemary and 4 fresh bayleaves (optional)

Method

Chop the dried fruit finely and place in a large mixing bowl. Peel and grate the apples pouring away any excess juice and add to the dried fruit. Add all the seasonings and mix. Add the two eggs and mix again to blend all the ingredients. At this stage the stuffing may look too sloppy – don't worry as the eggs will bind it during the cooking.

Remove the turkey from its packaging and untruss. Remove giblets, etc., from the neck- and leg-end cavities. Place a small amount of butter in the base of a roasting dish which is large enough to hold the turkey easily but not too large. Roast vegetables must be cooked in a separate dish. Place the turkey in the dish and push the stuffing into both ends of the bird, folding down the flap of skin at the neck end to hold the stuffing in, and pinning the leg end with cocktail sticks. Sprinkle all over with garlic granules. Place slices of butter all over the breast and legs. Arrange the bayleaves and rosemary over the breast. Cover loosely with foil and put in a slow oven (150°C, 300°F, gas mark 2) for 4 hours.

After the first hour, remove the foil and baste. Do not replace the foil. Baste at least every hour throughout. Roast vegetables should be cooked on a rack above the turkey after the first hour. Add several tablespoons of pan drippings from the turkey to the vegetables. If you are not cooking roast vegetables, keep an eye on the turkey – if it appears to brown too much, the foil should be replaced.

Before serving, remove the turkey from the roasting dish and keep warm. The pan drippings in the roasting dish will contain browned bits of stuffing that has oozed out during the cooking, which help to make a delicious gravy. Tilt the roasting dish, skim off as much fat as possible, replace over a low heat, scrape up the brownings and blend into the pan drippings. You don't need to add anything more to the gravy – it's delicious as is – but if you want to increase the quantity, now add any of the following: about 225 ml (8 fl oz) of water or either red or white wine, a teaspoon of honey-mustard, a tablespoon or so of Greek yoghurt, crème fraîche or double cream.

Bring the gravy to the boil and reduce slightly, stirring well. The gravy will appear slightly lumpy because of the stuffing bits. If you can't stand this, pour into blender and blend until smooth. Reheat and serve.

Pork with fruit

Ingredients   **Serves four**
  4 pork chops
  6 stoned prunes
  12 dried apricots
  2 sweet apples
  1–2 teaspoons garlic granules
  1 teaspoon dried mixed herbs
  1 teaspoon Heinz tomato sauce (or any other starch-free ketchup)
  wine glass white wine or water
  salt
  1 teaspoon whole black peppercorns
  oil for frying

Method
Remove all unwanted fat from the chops and sprinkle with the
garlic granules. Heat a small amount of oil in a frying pan and
brown the chops on each side. Remove them from the heat.
Place the chops in an oven-proof dish.

  Chop the prunes and apricots. Peel and grate the apples. Mix
the fruit together and layer it over the chops. Return the pan to
a low heat and add the peppercorns, tomato sauce and water or
wine. Stir, scraping the brownings from the pan and blend.
Add a pinch of salt.

  Pour the sauce over the chops and fruit. Cover with lid or foil
and cook in a moderate oven at 180°C (350°F or gas mark 4) for
1–1½ hours.

Loin of pork with milk

Ingredients   **Serves six**
  2 kg (4 lb) loin of pork
  75 g (3 oz) butter
  about 1.1 litres (2 pints) milk
  salt and pepper

Method

No pork crackling with this dish – the excess fat should be trimmed off and the pork should be boned. Dust the meat with salt and pepper and allow to stand for 30 minutes or so at room temperature.

Melt the butter in a deep, heavy cooking pan with a lid (Dutch oven). Place the meat in the pan and fry on all sides until golden brown. Add the milk, cover the pan and cook slowly over a moderate heat for about 2 hours or until meat is thoroughly cooked. The milk sauce will be creamy and thick and slightly brown in colour.

Remove the meat from the pan, place it on serving dish and keep warm. If desired, a teaspoon of garlic powder can be stirred into the milk sauce. Allow it to cook for a few minutes and serve with the meat.

Afelia

This is a favourite dish of well-known Greek chef, Sotos Achilleos.

Ingredients

about 200 g (8 oz) per person of pork fillet or boned loin or shoulder
enough dry red wine to nearly cover the meat
3 cloves garlic
1 teaspoon onion granules
1 tablespoon lemon juice
1 tablespoon honey
handful crushed coriander seeds
handful whole black peppercorns
salt to taste
olive oil
Greek yoghurt

Method

The correct Greek way of cooking this dish is to leave the fat on the meat. Of course you must please yourself – if you're worried about cholesterol, cut the fat off. Cut the pork into chunky cubes. Place in a glass, china or stainless-steel bowl – not aluminium.

Crush the garlic roughly – don't purée it – and add it to the wine with all the other ingredients. Stir to blend and pour over the meat. Marinate overnight.

Heat the olive oil over a medium heat. Remove the meat from the marinade with a slotted spoon, place in a frying pan with a lid and cook covered until the meat is browned and tender, stirring frequently. For the last 5 minutes of the cooking time, turn the heat low and toss the meat in the frying pan with lid on – Sotos swears this helps to tenderise the meat. Serve.

Sauce (optional)
Drain marinade to remove garlic and peppercorns. Return a cup or so of the drained marinade to the frying pan and stir into the meat brownings. Add a couple of tablespoons Greek yoghurt and stir to blend. Serve with the meat.

Pork fillet with orange

Ingredients   **Serves four**
  750 g (1½ lb) pork fillet
  garlic granules
  75 g (3 oz) butter
  150 ml (¼ pint) orange juice
  1 fresh orange
  4 tablespoons orange liqueur

Method
Remove any excess fat or gristle from the pork and slice it into inch-thick rounds and sprinkle lightly with garlic granules. Thinly peel the skin of the orange with a potato peeler, being careful to get only the orange zest and none of the bitter white pith, and cut into very fine matchstrip sticks. Squeeze the orange and add the juice to the 150 ml (¼ pint) of orange juice.

Melt the butter in a frying pan and add the pork, frying 2–3 minutes on each side. Remove the pork to a warm plate. Add the orange juice to the pan and simmer for a few minutes. Add the orange sticks and the orange liqueur. Simmer until the sauce begins to thicken. Return the pork to the pan, along with any juices, and continue to cook for one more minute. Serve with the sauce.

Baked gammon with mustard sauce

Ingredients   **Serves four to six**
1.25 kg (2½ lb) gammon
550 ml (1 pint) cider or apple juice
1–2 tablespoons soft brown sugar

Mustard Sauce (optional)
1 egg
2 teaspoons fruit sugar
2 teaspoons sharp Dijon mustard
4 tablespoons malt or white vinegar
1 cup liquid meat is cooked in
1 tablespoon Greek yoghurt or double cream
salt and pepper to taste

Method
Soak the gammon for 24 hours in cold water in the fridge. Drain and put it into a pan. Cover it with water again, bring to the boil and boil for 12 minutes. Remove from the heat and drain. Place the meat in a deep oven-proof dish, pour the cider or apple juice around it and bake for 1–1¼ hours in a moderate oven at 180°C (350°F or gas mark 4), basting with the juice. Take the meat from the oven, remove the skin but not the fat. Allow it to cool slightly then press sugar into the fat. Return to the oven for 30 minutes.

To make the mustard sauce, break the egg into a small saucepan, stir in the fruit sugar, the Dijon mustard and the vinegar. Begin to stir over a very low heat, slowly adding a cup of liquid from the meat, until the sauce begins to thicken. Stir in the yoghurt or cream and simmer until desired consistency is achieved. Adjust the seasonings. Remove the meat from the oven and serve with the sauce.

Pork and pears

Ingredients   **Serves two**
  2 *loin pork chops*
  2 *tablespoons olive oil*
  salt and freshly ground black pepper
  garlic granules
  2 *ripe pealed pears cut into slices*
  225 *ml (8 fl oz) apple juice*
  1 *tablespoon plain mild yoghurt*

Method
Sprinkle the chops with garlic granules, then heat the oil in
a frying pan and add the chops. Cook over a high heat on
both sides to seal the meat. Turn the heat down, add the pears
and cook for about 10–15 minutes until tender and browned.
Remove the chops and pears onto a warm plate. Pour any
excess fat from the pan, return to the heat and add the apple
juice. Scrape the brownings into the juice and stir well.
Simmer until reduced by about half. Add the yoghurt and
stir to blend. Add salt and pepper to taste. Pour over the
chops and serve.

Pork with marsala

Ingredients   **Serves four**
  750 *g (1½ lb) pork fillet*
  3 *tablespoons olive or sunflower oil*
  salt and pepper
  100 *ml (4 fl oz) marsala wine*

Method
Slice the pork fillet into inch-thick medallion slices, heat the oil
in a frying pan and brown quickly on both sides. Sprinkle with
salt and pepper, then pour in the marsala. Lower the heat a
little and cook for a few minutes until the meat is cooked
through and the liquid reduced.

Pork chops and apple crumble

Ingredients   **Serves two**
  2 loin pork chops
  2 teaspoons garlic powder
  30 g (1 oz) butter
  1 tablespoon cooking oil
  2 sweet eating apples such as Gala
  150 ml (¼ pint) apple juice or cider or white wine
  1 teaspoon honey-mustard
  salt and pepper
  75 g (3 oz) ground almonds
  125 g (3 oz) mild cooking cheese – Cheddar, Emmental, Gruyère
    or Jaalsburg, etc.

Method

Sprinkle the chops with garlic powder on both sides, melt the
butter and oil together in a frying pan and fry the chops until
lightly browned on both sides. Remove from the heat and place
the chops in a single layer in an oven-proof dish.

Peel and slice each cooking apple into eight slices. Return the
pan to the heat and quickly brown apples on both sides in the
pan juices. Remove the pan from the heat and layer the apples
over the chops.

Return the pan to a low heat, add the honey-mustard and
juice or cider or wine. Stir well to blend the pan brownings.
Pour over the apples and chops. Cover and cook in a moderate
oven at 180°C (350°F or gas mark 4) for 45 minutes.

Meanwhile, grate the cheese and mix with the ground
almonds. Take the chops from the oven, uncover and pour the
cheese and almond mixture over. Return to the oven and cook
for a further 15 minutes or until the top is brown and the cheese
bubbling.

Roast beef

Slow roasting beef until rare or just medium is better for
today's lean cuts of meat to ensure juicier, more tender results.
For topside or silverside, set the oven to 140°C, 275°F, gas mark
1 and cook for about 40 minutes per pound or 90 minutes per
kilogram. However, the shape of a roast may cause variation in

cooking time. A rolled, tied roast may be thicker and take an extra 10 minutes per pound (500 grams). Usually, instead of sprinkling the roast with flour, I sprinkle with dried garlic granules and sometimes coat with Dijon pepper mustard. Here's another successful idea.

Ingredients
   1.5 kg (3 lb) topside beef
   2 cloves garlic
   2 tablespoons whole peppercorns
   1 tablespoon dried oregano
   1 tablespoon olive oil

Method
Wipe the meat and pat dry. Peel the garlic and with a sharp knife, slice into small slivers. Make small slits all over the roast with the knife and insert a garlic slice into each.

Coarsely crush the peppercorns by placing them between two sheets of waxed paper or into a plastic food bag, and crushing with a food mallet or rolling pin. You can buy cracked peppercorns but the flavour of freshly crushed is better. Coarsely ground pepper is too strong. Discard the top sheet of paper or slit the food bag open, then mix in dried oregano.

Brush the meat with oil and roll in the peppercorn mixture until coated on all sides. Place on a greased rack in a roasting pan. Roast, as above, for 2 hours or until meat thermometer registers 60°C or 140°F for rare or 70°C, 160°F for medium. Remove from the oven and stand on a serving dish in warm place for 15 minutes, lightly covered with foil. Make gravy as described in 'Sauces' section on page 194.

Hamburgers galore

Basic ingredients   Serves two
   225 g (8 oz) minced beef – not too lean, as this makes the burger
      too dry
   salt and freshly ground black pepper
   30 g (1 oz) butter
   1 tablespoon cooking oil

Method

Mix beef with a sprinkling of salt (not too much) and pepper, and mould into two patties. Heat the butter and oil in a frying pan, when sizzling, fry the burgers on both sides until crisp and springy to the touch – 3–4 minutes for rare burgers, longer for well done. Remove from the heat, keep warm, add 4 tablespoons of water to the pan, mix with the pan drippings and a teaspoon Dijon mustard. Serve over burgers.

Add these variations to the ground beef basic recipe:

- 2 tablespoons each of grated cheese and chopped parsley.
- A lump of blue cheese about the size of a walnut, stuffed in the middle of the burger.
- A tablespoon double cream with $\frac{1}{2}$ teaspoon of garlic granules.
- 2 teaspoons mild Dijon mustard.
- 2 teaspoons dried herbs and a squeeze of lemon juice.

Fillet steak with garlic pepper

The most important hint I can offer about cooking steak is to buy the best steak you can afford. Nothing can replace quality – no amount of marinating or fancy sauces will really replace the wonderful texture and flavour of a quality steak. The best fillet has tiny threads of fat running through the meat, although with the present attitude to cholesterol, it is becoming harder and harder to find. Fillet steak is now very competitively priced by comparison to lamb, and you can eat almost every morsel, so it is not the extravagance it once was. Very simple cooking will suffice to do justice to a good fillet steak. This recipe includes fresh garlic slivers in the steak. The garlic does not cook enough to cause IBS problems – it simply warms through, imparting a delicate garlicy aroma through the meat.

Ingredients

thickish steak per person – at least 3–5 cm ($1\frac{1}{2}$–2 inches) thick
clove of garlic
olive oil
garlic granules
coarsley crushed peppercorns
red wine (optional)

Method

Trim the steaks of any unnecessary fat or sinew. Peel the garlic and slice into slivers. Make small cuts in each steak and slip a sliver of garlic into each. Sprinkle one side with garlic granules and a little crushed pepper.

Heat a little oil in a heavy-based frying pan. Place each steak pepper-side down and cook quickly over a high heat, without burning. Sprinkle garlic granules and pepper over the uncooked side, turn and cook.

If you want medium rare, medium or well-done steaks, turn down the heat and cook uncovered until the meat looks about right when pierced with a sharp knife. This is a matter of personal taste and judgement – no amount of clock-watching will give you the right result. Remove the steak just before you think the colour inside is about right. Place the steaks on a warm plate and de-glaze the pan juices with a slosh of red wine if you wish – this is entirely optional. You can also add a little mustard or salt to taste, or you can simply serve the steaks without anything else.

Fillet in the piece with creamy peppercorn sauce

This is an extravagance – at least in this country – but it is sensationally delicious. I long for the day when fillet steak will become as cheap as it is in Australia and then this dish would be about the same price as a Sunday roast of lamb. You will need half a fillet and it doesn't really matter which end of the fillet you choose – ask your butcher to advise you.

Ingredients   **Serves six**

½ *a whole beef fillet*
2–3 cloves garlic
garlic granules
olive oil
2–3 tablespoons mild whole seed or peppercorn mustard
100–225 ml (4–8 fl oz) cup red wine
1 teaspoon mustard extra
2–3 tablespoons cream (optional)

Method

Trim the fillet of surplus fat, gristle or sinew, especially the tough silvery layer along the top, which should be carefully 'skinned' off, using a very sharp knife: slide the blade of the knife under the skin and pull towards you, cutting as close to the skin as possible. Peel the garlic cloves and slice into thin slivers. Stud the fillet with the slivers of garlic by making slits all over with the point of a sharp knife and inserting a sliver into each.

Pour a very little oil into the bottom of a roasting dish, brush the fillet with oil and place in the roasting dish. Sprinkle one side with garlic granules and spread with mustard. Turn over and repeat so that the fillet is completely covered with mustard, including the ends.

Place in a hot oven (230°C, 450°F, gas mark 8) for 5 minutes. Reduce the heat to 180°C (350°F, gas mark 4) and cook for about 25 minutes for rare meat or longer if preferred – slip the point of a sharp knife into the middle of the fillet and see how rare it looks. Remove just before desired 'doneness' and place on a warm plate.

Tilt the roasting pan, skim off the fat, return the pan to the heat and add the mustard and wine. Stir into the pan drippings and boil for a few seconds. Add cream if desired and serve with the fillet, which may be sliced thinly like roast beef or in thick 'fillet mignon' sized pieces

Carpet bag steaks downunder

In America they call this 'Surf 'n' Turf', but the idea originated in Sydney, Australia. Steaks can be filled with oysters several hours ahead and kept covered in a refrigerator.

Ingredients   **Serves four**

16 oysters
1 tablespoon lemon juice
4 thick fillet steaks
50 g (2 oz) melted butter
100 ml (4 fl oz) red wine
2 teaspoons Dijon wholegrain mustard
30 g (1 oz) butter extra

Method

Combine the oysters and lemon juice in a small bowl and marinate for at least 15 minutes. Cut a small pocket in the side of each steak and fill with the oysters. Secure the openings with cocktail sticks. Brush the steaks with butter and cook in a frying pan over a high heat, turning frequently and brushing with more butter during cooking, until cooked as desired.

Remove the steaks to a warm plate. Pour the wine into the pan, scrape the pan drippings and blend. Add the mustard and simmer for a few seconds. Add the extra butter, blend and serve over the steak.

Meatballs in sour cream sauce

Ingredients   **Serves 2**

350 g (12 oz) minced beef
1 teaspoon onion granules
1 teaspoon garlic granules
1 tablespoon starch-free tomato ketchup
1 tablespoon wholegrain Dijon mustard
½ teaspoon Greek mustard with black olives (optional)
1 tablespoon dried mixed herbs
2 eggs
2 tablespoons oil
225 ml (8 fl oz) water or 100 ml (4 fl oz) wine and 100 ml (4 fl oz)
    water or 225 ml (8 fl oz) apple juice
1 teaspoon honey-mustard
100 ml (4 fl oz) soured cream
salt and pepper

Method

Combine the first eight ingredients and mix well. Shape into smallish balls, place on a plate in a single layer and refrigerate for 30 minutes. Heat the oil in a frying pan over a medium heat, add the meatballs and cook gently until well browned all over and cooked through. Do not cover during cooking as this will make the meatballs fall apart. Remove from the pan and keep warm.

Pour any excess fat or oil from the pan. Return to the heat. Add the water/wine/juice and scrape down the pan brownings. Add the honey-mustard and bring to the boil and reduce a little. Stir in the soured cream, blend well, adjust the seasonings and return the meatballs to sauce. Simmer uncovered until heated through. Serve.

Beef cacciatore

I have included several recipes made with tomatoes but before you decide to try them, read my notes about tomatoes at the beginning of the soups section. This recipe makes a wonderful sauce for Bolognaise, lasagne or cacciatore, which is a pot-roast. Pot-roasting is another name for braising, and is ideal for chuck steak or blade steak as better cuts tend to become too dry. But it's not always easy to get chuck steak or blade steak in a large piece, and the magic of a pot-roast is being able to carve the meat, dripping in delicious savoury juices, while serving the sauce separately. I have often used silverside when unable to get a solid piece of braising steak.

Ingredients   **Serves six**

1.5 kg (3 lb) piece of beef – braising steak or silverside
2 tablespoons oil
2–3 teaspoons whole black peppercorns
2–3 fresh bayleaves
3–4 tablespoons dried onion flakes
3 teaspoons garlic granules
300 ml ($\frac{1}{2}$ pint) dry red or white wine
1$\frac{1}{2}$ tablespoons vinegar
300 ml ($\frac{1}{2}$ pint) water
100 ml (4 fl oz) jellied chicken stock (optional)
1 teaspoon dried basil
1 tablespoon dried mixed Italian/Mediterranean herbs
1–2 teaspoons fruit sugar
75 g (3 oz) butter
500 g (1 lb) fresh peeled tomatoes or 450 ml (16 fl oz) tomato juice
3 anchovy fillets
2 tablespoons milk
50 g (2 oz) stoned black olives
1 tablespoon chopped parsley

Method

Trim the surplus fat off the meat. Heat the oil in a large deep oven-proof dish or 'Dutch oven'. Add the meat and brown on all sides. Remove the meat and set aside.

Throw in the peppercorns and bayleaves and cook until peppercorns begin to pop (a few seconds) then add very quickly the wine and the vinegar. Boil until reduced by half, then add the water and the chicken stock and stir over the heat for about 2 minutes.

Blend or sieve the tomatoes if necessary, and pour into the pan. Add the onions, garlic granules, herbs and sugar, then boil all together for a few moments, stirring well. Add the butter and stir until blended then taste the mixture. If you think it needs more salt or sugar, add at this stage.

Return the meat to the pan, cover and cook in a moderate oven at 180°C (350°F or gas mark 4) for 1 to $1\frac{1}{2}$ hours until tender. Meanwhile, soak the anchovy fillet in milk and cut the olives in half. Remove the meat and stand on a warm plate. Drain the anchovies, chop them finely and add to the sauce, with the olives and parsley. Reheat and simmer for a minute. At this stage the meat can be returned to the sauce to await serving – just stand over a very low heat so that it is just keeping warm.

Carve the meat and serve the sauce separately. Serve with noodles or mashed potato for the family or visitors.

Lasagne

This is a way of making proper lasagne for the rest of the family and a small mock lasagne for yourself in a separate dish. You will need a Bolognaise sauce made either from your own recipe or use the recipe for beef cacciatore, substituting 1.5 kg (3 lb) of mince instead of the braising steak. You can either make half the recipe or make up the whole amount, and freeze half for another occasion. Both the sauce and the finished lasagne freeze well. If you want a less rich sauce, omit the anchovies and olives and add more water.

Ingredients   Serves three to four

Bolognaise sauce made with 750 g ($1\frac{1}{2}$ lb) mince
1 packet dried lasagne pasta, spinach or plain, or same amount
  fresh

750 g (1½ lb) cottage cheese
2 eggs
2 tablespoons chopped parsley
75 g (3 oz) grated Parmesan cheese
225 g (8 oz) mild grated cheese
2 teaspoons salt
freshly ground black pepper

Method

Have ready a large oblong lasagne pan and a small oven-proof dish for yourself. Lightly butter both dishes.

In a large mixing bowl beat the eggs, add the cottage cheese and blend well. Mix in the Parmesan cheese, parsley and 1 cup of mild grated cheese. Add salt and grind in some pepper.

Place a layer of lasagne on the bottom of the large dish – if you are using dried pasta, dip the strips in a dish of warm water before layering. Spread a layer of meat sauce over, then a layer of cottage cheese sauce, then repeat with pasta, meat sauce and cottage cheese, finishing with cottage cheese.

Leave enough meat and cheese sauce for yourself. Spread the desired amount of meat sauce in the small dish and top with cottage cheese. Sprinkle the remaining grated cheese over both dishes. Cook in a moderate oven at 180°C (350°F or gas mark 4) until bubbling and beginning to brown on top. Serve with a salad.

Old-fashioned roast lamb with real mint sauce

Ingredients   Serves four to six

1 good-sized leg – at least 2¼ kg (4½ lb)
several cloves garlic
several sprigs fresh rosemary (optional)
garlic granules to sprinkle
beef dripping or lard or a mixture of olive oil and butter

Method

The lamb should be completely covered with a thin layer of fat, which is necessary to keep in the juices. Wipe and pat dry. With a sharp knife, slice the ends off the garlic cloves, slip the skins off and slice each one into several slim slivers. Make deep slits all over the lamb with the point of the knife, inserting the garlic as you go, and a leaf or so of the rosemary. Dust the leg with garlic granules.

Melt the dripping, lard or oil and butter in a roasting pan to cover the bottom. Place the lamb in the pan, tilt the pan so that the fat runs to one side and baste the lamb thinly with the fat. Place in a slow to moderate oven (150°C–180°C, 300°F–350°F, gas mark 2–4) and roast for 30–35 minutes to the pound (500 g) – over two hours. This will produce an old-fashioned well-done roast. If you want a modern slightly rarer roast, cook in a moderate oven for 20 minutes to the pound (500 g) with 20 minutes over. Baste the meat several times during the cooking. A roasting bag can be used but this tends to braise the meat, rather than roast it.

Real Mint Sauce

Pick enough fresh mint to make 3–4 tablespoons when chopped. Wash the mint well, shake dry and strip the leaves. Discard the stalks, place the leaves on a chopping board and sprinkle with a tablespoon of ordinary granulated sugar. Begin to chop with a large sharp knife – the size of a carving knife. Hold the tip of the blade in one hand and the handle of the knife in the other, and chop up and down, scraping the mint into the centre again as it rolls out to the edge.

Sprinkle with another tablespoon of sugar and keep chopping until the mint is very fine and pulpy. Scrape into a serving jug and barely cover with boiling water and about 100 ml (4 fl oz) of vinegar – either white or malt. Stir a few times and leave to steep. Serve with the lamb.

Glazed leg of lamb

Guaranteed to produce a deliciously tender roast with wonderful flavour and a marvellous gravy.

Quince jam is the best for this recipe, but is not always readily available. Do not use jelly jam, as it is too slippery to coat the lamb properly and slides off. The jam glaze does not produce a particularly sweet flavour, as you might think, but acts as a tenderising marinade.

Ingredients   Serves eight

1 large leg of lamb
1 or 2 jars best red currant, quince or apricot jam
two cloves garlic (optional)
olive oil

Method

Line a roasting tin with sheets of foil, making sure there are no slits in the foil so that the meat and jam juices cannot escape into the roasting pan during the cooking. Lightly oil the foil base. If using garlic (it has never caused me IBS problems used like this) remove skins and slice into slivers. Make deep slits all over the lamb with the point of a knife, inserting the garlic as you go. Score the top of the lamb lightly with a diamond pattern. Spread with the jam, place in the foil and wrap around. Bake in a moderate oven 180°C (350°F or gas mark 4) for about $2\frac{1}{2}$ hours, basting occasionally during the cooking.

Unwrap the foil, spread some more jam over the meat and bake for a further 30–45 minutes, uncovered. Remove the meat to a warm serving plate. Carefully lift the foil from the roasting pan, pouring all the juices back into the pan. Discard the foil. Tilt the pan and allow the fat to rise to the top. Skim the fat off with a large spoon. Place the pan over a low heat and simmer until the juices are reduced. You will not need to add anything extra to this gravy. If you think it needs diluting, you could add water and perhaps a little cream, but it is best just as it comes. The joint is equally delicious hot or cold.

Des Brittain's lamb

Ingredients   Serves four

whole loin of lamb, boned, including fillet
several sprigs of fresh rosemary
1–2 teaspoons garlic granules
30 g (1 oz) melted butter
3 tablespoons red currant jelly
1 teaspoon mild Dijon mustard

Method

Ask the butcher to bone the lamb for you or do it yourself: first cut off the fillet, then with a sharp knife slice down inside of the bones along the loin. Discard the bones, fat and skin.

Pull the rosemary leaves off their sprigs and chop roughly. Spread the loin open, lie the fillet in the middle, brush with butter, then sprinkle with rosemary and garlic granules. Roll up the lamb and tie with string.

Cook in an open roasting dish or oven-proof pan in a moderate oven at 180°C (350°F or gas mark 4) for 40–50 minutes or until cooked as desired. Turn off the oven and leave for about 10 minutes.

In a small saucepan mix the red currant jelly with the mustard and heat together. Slice the lamb into thick 'fillet mignon' sized pieces and spoon the sauce over the meat.

Rack of lamb with mint bernaise

Ingredients   **Serves four**
  4 racks of lamb with 3 chops in each
  2 tablespoons French mustard
  1 tablespoon oil

Mint Bernaise
  75 ml (2½ fl oz) white vinegar
  ½ teaspoon garlic granules
  6 black peppercorns
  4 egg yolks
  250 g (9 oz) butter
  ½ cup mint leaves firmly packed

Method
Ask the butcher to trim the loin chops to make the racks or buy a loin with the right amount of chops in it and trim off the excess fat so that each chop has a couple of inches of bone exposed. Cut down between the chops to allow a rack of three per person.

Spread the mustard over each rack, covering the remaining fat on the top and the underside. Pour a very little oil into a roasting dish and stand the racks on end, balancing them against each other. Roast in a moderate oven at 180°C (350°F or gas mark 4) for 20–25 minutes for rare meat, longer if desired.

Melt the butter and set aside to cool slightly. Place the vinegar, garlic granules and peppercorns in a small saucepan and bring to the boil. Boil rapidly until reduced by half. Strain the liquid into the top of double boiler or a bowl set in a saucepan of simmering water. Add the egg yolks and beat with an electric beater over the simmering water for 1 minute. Add the cooled melted butter gradually, continuing to beat until thickened. Remove from the heat, place in a blender with the mint leaves and blend for 30 seconds. Serve over the lamb.

Everyday meals

Quick, easy and economical for lunch or supper.

Bacon star

Ingredients   Serves two
200 g (1½ lb) bacon rashers
1–2 sweet apples, depending on size
6 oz mild cheese – Emmental, Gruyère, Jaalsburg, Cheddar –
  whatever you prefer as long as it's mild

Method
Lay the bacon rashers in a large shallow oven-proof dish and
put it in a hot oven at 200°C (400°F or gas mark 6). I use a large
quiche dish and arrange the bacon in a cartwheel design. Peel
and grate the apple. Grate the cheese. Remove the partly cooked
bacon from the oven and cover with a layer of apple and top
with the grated cheese. Return to the oven and cook until the
cheese is melted and beginning to brown – about 20 minutes.
This can be eaten as a cold savoury, sliced into fingers. It is very
handy for taking as a snack, when travelling.

Simple braised steak

Ingredients   Serves four to five
1 kg (2 lb) chuck steak
2 tablespoons dried onion flakes
1 teaspoon garlic granules
salt and freshly ground pepper
100 ml (4 fl oz) claret or water
1 tablespoon chopped parsley (optional)

Method
Trim any gristle or fat from the steak and cut into serving size
pieces. Mix the dried onions and garlic powder together on a
dinner plate and press the steak onto the mixture, turning and
coating each side liberally. Place in a casserole dish and sprinkle
any remaining dried vegetables over the meat. Season with salt
and pepper to taste. Pour the water or claret over and cover the
casserole with a lid or tightly with foil. Bake in a moderate oven

at 180°C (350°F or gas mark 4) for 1½ hours or until tender.

Don't be tempted to add more liquid in the initial stages of cooking – the meat juices and the dried onions combine together with the small amount of liquid to form a luscious gravy.

Grandma's rissoles

Ingredients   **Serves four**

about 500 g (1 lb) leftover roast beef
2 eggs
4 tablespoons chopped parsley
2 teaspoons Dijon pepper mustard
1 tablespoon non-starch vinaigrette dressing
1 tablespoon Heinz tomato sauce
1 tablespoon dried onion granules

Method

Mince the beef, add the other ingredients and mix well, or process everything in a food processor, adding the beef first and chopping roughly, then the other ingredients. Spoon into patty tins and cook in a moderate oven at 180°C (350°F or gas mark 4) for about 30 minutes.

Alternatively, squeeze small handfuls together, roll in a mixture of ground almonds and garlic powder and fry in hot oil until brown.

Frankfurter sauté

Ingredients   **Serves two to three**

10 pack Herta skinless frankfurters (or any starch-free
    frankfurters)
1 tablespoon dried onions
1 sweet apple
5–6 whole peppercorns (optional)
3 tablespoons Greek yoghurt
1 tablespoon cooking oil
2 teaspoons Heinz tomato ketchup
2 teaspoons Dijon mustard

Method
Cube the frankfurters. Peel, core and cube the apples. Heat the oil in a frying pan over a medium heat, add onions and peppercorns and sauté for 2 minutes. Add the apples and sauté for two minutes. Add the frankfurters and lightly brown. Mix the yoghurt with the tomato ketchup and mustard. Pour over the frankfurters and cook over a low heat, stirring occasionally until the sauce is brown and thick. Serve.

Shredded turnip gratin

I have not tried this dish recently – I used to make it years ago, before I discovered I was starch-intolerant. Since I have discovered that both turnips and swedes have a very low starch rating and should not cause IBS symptoms, I have added it to the book, but if you think it causes any problems, don't repeat it. It can be made with either turnips, swedes or with a mixture of both and tastes quite delicious.

Ingredients
 750 g (1½ lb) tender turnips and/or swedes
 125 g 1(4½ oz) butter
 salt and pepper to taste
 1 teaspoon fruit sugar
 150 ml (¼ pint) double cream
 125 g (4 oz) grated mild cheese

Method
Peel and grate the turnips and/or swedes. Melt the butter in a frying pan and add the grated vegetables. Fry gently over a low heat turning frequently, trying not to brown. After about 10 minutes, sprinkle with the salt and fruit sugar, stir to blend well, remove and place in a buttered gratin dish. Pour over the cream and season generously with pepper. Top with the grated cheese and bake in a moderate to hot oven at 190°C (375°F or gas mark 5) until bubbling and beginning to brown.

Quick gammon bake

Ingredients   **Serves one**
1 large slice cooked gammon or ham
1 teaspoon mild sweet Dijon or any starch-free mustard
1 small eating apple
1–2 slices processed cheese

Method
Spread the mustard over the ham. Peel and slice the apple.
Lay it over the ham, then place the cheese over the apple.
Grill or cook in a hot oven at 200°C (400°F or gas mark 6)
until the cheese is brown and bubbling.

Cheese and bacon cream

Ingredients   **Serves two**
125 g (½ cup) medium Cheddar or Swiss-type cheese, grated
225 ml (8 fl oz) whipping cream
1 egg beaten
2 rashers bacon

Method
Dice and fry the bacon gently until cooked but not crisp.
Combine with the other ingredients and pour into a buttered
oven-proof dish. Bake in a moderate oven at 180°C (350°F or
gas mark 4) for 20 minutes.

Spicy haddock steaks

Ingredients   **Serves one**
1–2 haddock steaks, fresh or defrosted frozen
30 g (1 oz) butter
1 tablespoon lemon juice
2 teaspoons Heinz or any starch-free tomato ketchup
1 teaspoon sweet Dijon mustard

Sauce
½ clove crushed garlic
1 teaspoon sweet Dijon mustard
150 g (5 oz) mild low-fat yoghurt

Method
In a small saucepan, melt the butter, then add the lemon juice, tomato ketchup and mustard. Heat through gently – don't worry if the mixture curdles. Remove from the heat.

Brush the fish steaks with the mixture on one side. Cook under a hot grill or in a hot oven at 200°C (400°F or gas mark 6) for about 5 minutes. Remove from the heat, turn and brush the other side of the fish with the mixture. Continue cooking for another 5 minutes. Meanwhile, blend the garlic, mustard and yoghurt. Serve sauce cold with fish.

Frittata

Ingredients   **Serves four**
  6 *eggs*
  4 *tablespoons onion flakes*
  400 g (14 oz) *whole peeled tomatoes*
  30 g (1 oz) *butter*
  1 *tablespoon cooking oil*
  3 *slices ham*
  1 *tablespoon chopped parsley*
  ½ *teaspoon fresh or dried basil*
  2 *tablespoons grated Parmesan cheese*

Method
Chop the tomatoes roughly. Finely chop the ham, parsley and basil, and combine in a large bowl with the tomatoes, onions and Parmesan cheese. Whisk the eggs, then pour over the tomato mixture and blend well.

Melt the butter and oil together in a shallow pan. Pour in the mixture and cook over a very low heat for about 10 minutes, without stirring. Place the pan under a hot grill or in a hot oven at 200°C (400°F or gas mark 6) until the mixture is set. Do not let the top brown. Cut into wedges and serve with a salad. This can also be eaten cold.

Broccoli amandine

Ingredients   **Serves four to six**
1 kg (2$\frac{1}{4}$ lb) broccoli
pinch fruit sugar
lemon juice
40 g (1$\frac{1}{2}$ oz) slivered blanched almonds
60 g (2$\frac{1}{2}$ oz) unsalted butter
1 teaspoon garlic powder
salt and pepper to taste

Method
Trim the outside leaves and tough stems from the broccoli, break or cut into chunky flowerettes and cook in a small amount of salted boiling water with a pinch of fruit sugar. Remove from the heat when broccoli is still slightly crisp. Drain and place in a hot serving dish, then squeeze with a little lemon juice. Melt the butter in a frying pan, add the almonds, sprinkle the garlic powder over and brown lightly. Pour the butter and almonds over the broccoli and serve. Add pepper to taste.

Puffed cheese fish

Ingredients   **Serves three to four**
6 medium fillets white fish
salt and pepper
2–3 tablespoons cooking oil
100 ml (4 fl oz) starch-free mayonnaise
125 g (4 oz) grated mild-medium Cheddar
1 tablespoon chopped parsley
1 teaspoon lemon juice
1 stiffly beaten egg white

Method
Wash and dry the fish, sprinkle with salt and lightly brown on both sides in the cooking oil. Remove from the heat, drain and lay the fish in a buttered oven-proof dish. Combine the remaining ingredients and pile over the fish fillets. Bake in a moderate oven at 180°C (350°F or gas mark 4) for 12 minutes or until the coating is puffed and browned.

Tomato cheesy scrambled eggs for one

Ingredients
2 eggs
25 g butter
75 ml (2½ fl oz) milk (approximately)
handful grated cheese
pinch salt
1 beefsteak tomato, sliced thickly
freshly ground black pepper

Method
Beat the eggs with a fork, then add the milk and salt. Melt
the butter in a frying pan over a low heat and pour in the
eggs. Cook very slowly, until just beginning to set. Throw
the cheese onto the eggs and cook a few more seconds until
set. Remove from the heat, then pile the eggs onto the sliced
tomatoes, season with pepper and eat.

Tomato and peppered cottage cheese salad for one

Ingredients
1 large beefsteak tomato
small pack of cottage cheese
½ teaspoon fruit sugar
½ teaspoon salt
½ teaspoon garlic granules
freshly ground black pepper
starch-free steak seasoning

Method
Cut the tomato in half. Sprinkle each half with the fruit sugar,
salt, garlic granules and ground black pepper. Pile the cottage
cheese onto each half and sprinkle with a little steak
seasoning. Chopped chives may also be added.

Baked apple savoury

Ingredients   **Serves one**
> 1 large sweet apple
> 1 Herta frankfurter
> 2 teaspoons butter
> 1 teaspoon sweet Dijon mustard
> dash Heinz tomato ketchup

Method
Core the apple to make a hole big enough for the frankfurter.
Beat the butter, mustard and ketchup together. Spread on top
of the apple. Cook in a hot oven until tender.

Egg and spinach casserole

Ingredients   **Serves four**
> 1 kg (2¼ lb) spinach
> 75 g (3 oz) butter
> 2–3 eggs, beaten
> 2–3 tablespoons grated Parmesan cheese
> chopped marjoram (optional)
> salt and pepper to taste

Method
Pile the spinach into a sink full of water, stir and dunk in the
water until all leaves are washed, then leave to soak while the
sand sinks to the bottom. Remove the spinach, change the water
and repeat the process three times in all. This is very important as
spinach is grown in sand. It is also the reason pre-washed spinach
is so much dearer – and I think worth paying for!

Pile the leaves into a large saucepan, press down well, put the
lid on and cook unsalted and without additional water for 2–3
minutes or until tender. Remove from the heat, put a plate into
the saucepan, hold over the sink and press the plate down, drain-
ing the water away. Get the spinach as well-drained as possible.

Melt the butter in an oven-proof casserole dish, add the
spinach and season lightly with salt. Mix the beaten eggs with
the Parmesan cheese and the marjoram, pour over the spinach,
stir to blend and place in a hot oven at 200°C (400°F or gas mark
6) until the eggs are set.

Swedish beef olives

Ingredients   **Serves two**
350 g (12 oz) thinly sliced beef – topside, rump or chuck
2 large sweet apples
12 finely chopped dried apricots
6 chopped stoned prunes
2 tablespoons chopped parsley
2 teaspoons mixed dried herbs
1 tablespoon finely chopped pitted green olives (optional)
2 eggs
salt and pepper
30 g (1 oz) butter
1 tablespoon oil for cooking
2 teaspoons honey-mustard
100 ml (4 fl oz) water
wine glass of wine – red or white
2 tablespoons mild plain yoghurt

Method
You can buy thin slices of beef for beef olives in most supermarkets, but if you have to prepare it yourself, buy as lean a piece of meat as possible, and slice thinly with a very sharp knife into rectangles which will roll up when stuffed into the size of small sausages. Then beat the beef with the edge of a saucer or a meat mallet until as thin as possible, without making holes in the meat.

Peel and grate the apples and mix with the finely chopped dried fruit, herbs, parsley and olives. Beat the eggs and add to the fruit mixture. Season with salt to taste. Combine until well blended.

Put spoonfuls of mixture on each slice of beef and roll up. Secure with cocktail sticks or tie with string. Brown quickly on each side in a frying pan. Remove from the heat and place in a single layer in an oven-proof dish. Return the pan to the heat, add the honey-mustard, water, wine and yoghurt, and stir well to blend. Remove from the heat and pour over the beef olives. Cook in slow oven at 140°C (275°F or gas mark 1) for 1½ hours or until tender. They can be cooked in a very low oven or slow cooker for 3–4 hours.

Pork pockets

Ingredients   **Serves four**
4 good large thick pork chops or steaks
sprinkle of garlic granules
oil for frying
stuffing as for Swedish beef olives (see previous recipe)
325 ml (12 fl oz) orange juice

Method
Slice through the chops or steaks to create a pocket. Stuff with
the stuffing. If necessary, seal the edge with cocktail sticks.
Lightly sprinkle garlic granules over one side of the meat and
brown quickly, garlic side down, in oil in the frying pan.
Sprinkle garlic granules over the upper side and turn to brown.
Remove the pan from the heat and place the meat in a single
layer in an oven-proof dish. Return the pan to the heat, pour in
the orange juice and stir with the pan brownings, boil to reduce
slightly and pour over the meat. Cook in a moderate oven at
180°C (350°F or gas mark 4) for 1–1½ hours or until tender.

Gammon Jonathan

Ingredients   **Serves one to two**
1 large slice of ham or gammon – about 3 cm (1½ inches) thick
25 g (1 oz) butter
1 tablespoon fruit sugar or brown sugar
1 teaspoon strong Dijon mustard
small carton single cream

Method
Melt the butter in a frying pan and fry the ham lightly on both
sides. Mix the mustard and sugar. Remove the ham, spread on
one side with half the mustard mixture. Pour a little of the
single cream into a shallow oven-proof dish and place the ham,
mustard side down in this. Spread the remaining mustard
mixture on the top side of the ham, then pour more single
cream over to cover. Lay foil over the top to cover lightly. Bake
in a moderate oven at 180°C (350°F or gas mark 4) until very
tender – about 45 minutes to an hour.

Fish patties with lemon sauce

Ingredients   **Serves two**
750 g (1½ lb) white fish fillets
1 mild-tasting apple
1 egg
2 tablespoons chopped fresh chives
1 tablespoon fresh basil
1 tablespoon lemon juice
2 tablespoons cranberry or red currant jelly
1 teaspoon sweet Dijon mustard
oil or butter for greasing patty pans

Sauce
½ cup starch-free mayonnaise
2 tablespoons chopped fresh chives
1 tablespoon lemon juice

Method
Skin and bone the fish fillets. Peel and core the apple. Either finely chop the fish, grate apple then mix with the other ingredients or process until fine but not mushy. Grease eight patty pans (either rub around with a butter paper or put a drop of oil into the bottom of each and rub around with cooking paper) and press spoonfuls of the fish mixture into each patty pan and cook in a moderate oven at 180°C (350°F or gas mark 4) for about 45 minutes or until the top is beginning to brown.

Meanwhile, blend the mayonnaise, chives and lemon juice. Serve the patties with the sauce.

Scrambled sausage cups

Ingredients   **Serves one**
2 eggs
75 ml (2½ fl oz) milk
75 g (3 oz) butter
salt and freshly ground black pepper
2–3 slices of German garlic sausage or mild salami or other
    starch-free sausage
1 large tomato

Method
Beat the eggs lightly with the milk. Season with salt and pepper. Melt two thirds of the butter in a heavy pan set on a very low heat. Pour in the egg mixture and cook covered, very slowly. Use a heat mat underneath if possible, to prevent browning on bottom.

Meanwhile, cook the sausage in a separate pan in the remainder of the butter until the edges curl up and become cup-shaped. Slice the tomato. When the eggs are cooked, place the sausage on a warmed plate, pile the eggs into each sausage cup and top with the sliced tomato, sprinkled with freshly ground black pepper.

Anzac omelette

Ingredients   **Serves one**
   2 eggs
   100 g (3½ oz) tin smoked oysters
   25 g (1 oz) butter
   2 tablespoons milk or single cream

Method
Drain the oysters, then rinse and chop them roughly. Separate the eggs. Beat the whites stiffly. Mix the yolks with the milk or cream and add the chopped oysters. Fold the whites into the mixture. Melt the butter in a frying pan or omelette pan, pile the mixture into the pan and cook without stirring until almost set. Brown under a grill. Fold in half and serve.

Baked supper savoury

Ingredients
   2 eggs per person
   approximately 75 g (3 oz) cheese per person
   milk or single cream
   butter
   salt and pepper

Method
Butter an oven-proof dish well and line the bottom and sides with grated cheese. Break in the eggs, pour the cream or milk

over, and season with salt and pepper. Either top with more
grated cheese or bake uncovered in a hot oven at 190°C (375°F
or gas mark 5) for 15–20 minutes

Denver ham patties

Ingredients   Serves one
1 cup minced leftover ham
12 g (½ oz or about 2 teaspoons) melted butter
2 tablespoons cranberry or redcurrant jelly
1 tablespoon chopped parsley
1 beaten egg

Method
For each person blend one portion of the ingredients. Press the
mixture into greased patty pans (about two to three patties per
person). Set the pans in a large pan of hot water, in a hot oven
at 190°C (375°F or gas mark 5). Cook for 15–20 minutes, or until
set. This can also be made with leftover turkey but will need
salt and pepper added to the mixture to taste.

Alternative cheese bake

Ingredients   Serves two
German sausage or frankfurters
3 eggs
250 g (9 oz) mild grated cheese
¾ pint milk
salt and pepper
further 125 g (4½ oz) grated cheese

Method
Slice the sausage or frankfurters and line a shallow buttered
oven-proof dish. Combine the next three ingredients, season
with salt and pepper to taste and pour over the sausage.
Sprinkle the further cheese over, stand the dish in a larger pan
of water, place in a moderate oven at 180°C (350°F or gas mark
4) and bake until set (about 20–30 minutes).

Salads

I eat at least one salad every day. Raw vegetables and fruit are the best source of fibre – and besides, I love them. You really have to eat lots of salads on the Sinclair Diet System so if you've always thought of salads as simply a couple of lettuce leaves and a tasteless tomato, think again. Learn to seek out the freshest and best-tasting vegetables. Don't buy when they're flabby and stale for the simple reason that they don't taste good.

Nowadays there are lovely sweet tomatoes and crisp, sweet, red peppers in the shops all year round. There's a huge variety of lettuce and herbs available – be adventurous, try things you're not familiar with.

If you've steered clear of real vinaigrettes for years because of the extra calories, now you can begin enjoying them again with a clear conscience. On the Sinclair Diet System you need the oil to compensate for the lack of the butter or margarine you used to eat on or with bread and cakes.

Olive oil is especially high in the healthy polyunsaturated fats which we are all urged to eat more of. It is also particularly noted for its purity, which means that it doesn't need to be chemically purified, unlike most other oils, which go through a number of refining processes including neutralizing with caustic soda, 'washing and drying', bleaching and deodorising. I wholeheartedly recommend cold pressed virgin olive oil (first pressing) for its delicious flavour, both in cooking and in salad dressings. There are many varieties now available.

If you want to use ready-made vinaigrettes (and I often do) look for those which don't contain modified starch. I regret that these are becoming increasingly rare, even in France, the home of the vinaigrette. Most of the ready-made low-fat, oil-free dressings and vinaigrettes contain modified starch or maize starch. Freshly made starch-free vinaigrettes made with olive oil are sometimes available in the chilled foods section of your supermarkets.

Store salad carefully and it will stay fresh for longer

When you're making salad frequently you need a variety of ingredients to offset possible boredom. And if you're making it only for yourself, it's a problem to get through them before they go stale. Correct storage is important. Most lettuces are wrapped or sold in plastic bags these days. When you begin to use it, remove the lettuce from the wrapping, discard the outer leaves, remove the leaves you plan to use and wash well. Don't wash the rest of the lettuce at this stage unless it is very dirty, as this will slightly damage the leaves and cause lettuce 'rust' and slime. Don't put it back in the original wrapper as this may be dirty. Store in a fresh plastic bag in your refrigerator. Sprinkle a little water into the bag on the leaves and they should keep well for almost a week.

Store tomatoes, peppers, radishes and cucumbers unwashed and leave any stalks on until just before use. Store celery and carrots unwashed, but do discard tough outer celery stalks. The other half of an onion stores well for a couple of days in the refrigerator, covered in food-wrap.

Some herbs such as parsley store better after washing, but they must be drained well and stored in a plastic bag. Herbs with delicate leaves, such as rocket and basil, tend to wilt quickly, but don't react well to a rough washing. Don't disturb them unless they're looking very jaded. Use them soon after buying or buy in the pots and water as instructed.

Mushrooms are best left undisturbed in their original packs. Buy small amounts, remove those you want to use and return the rest to the fridge. Brown paper bags are often recommended for mushrooms, but I honestly don't think it makes any difference.

Bags of pre-washed mixed salad are more expensive and don't last as well, but save space in your refrigerator.

Simple green salad

I never get tired of a mixture of greens and herbs with a good dressing. Best made every day but you can make enough for two days and store the rest in a bowl, covered with cling-wrap, in the fridge.

Ingredients

at least two different types of leaf: cos (romaine), iceberg (crisphead), little gem, bronze, oakleaf, lollo rosso, endive, Chinese cabbage, chicory or spinach at least two different types of herbs: parsley, chives, rocket, watercress, mustard and cress, Lamb's lettuce, dandelion

Method

Select for a variety of colour and shape. Wash the lettuce leaves, tear into bite-sized pieces or use whole. Wash the herbs and chop if necessary. Place in a larger, wider bowl than looks necessary and just before serving, add a dribble of good dressing and toss. This is really all you need, but I often add sliced mushrooms and several whole small tomatoes. The salad should look very leafy, with at most, only a few other additions for variety.

Simple coleslaw

I prefer to slice the cabbage because it has a milder taste, but some experts say the cabbage should be shredded, then soaked in ice-water for a few minutes, drained thoroughly and chilled. However you do it, a coleslaw can be as simple as:

Ingredients   **Serves four**

approximately 275 g (10 oz) or about 2–3 cups of finely shredded cabbage
100 ml (4 fl oz) any starch-free mayonnaise
1 tablespoon cream
salt and freshly ground black pepper

Method

Place cabbage in a salad bowl, sprinkle with a little salt and pepper, combine the mayonnaise with the cream and add little by little, tossing all the while. Just moisten cabbage – you may not need to use all the dressing.

To this basic recipe any or all of the following may be added. (Measurements are approximate only – use your own judgement.)

1 cup grated carrot
1 cup cut-up red apple with skin on
½ cup diced celery
½ cup diced red pepper
½ cup chopped parsley
½ cup chopped chives
½ cup diced dates

Grilled goat's cheese salad

The fresher the goat's cheese is, the milder it will be. My preference is for a mild, creamy taste, but it's entirely a matter of personal opinion.

Ingredients

1 goat's cheese about 10 cm (4 inches) thick for each person
green salad made from any combination of lettuce and herbs,
   including whole cherry tomatoes
black olives
capers
vinaigrette

Method

Make the salad and arrange in a large, shallow salad bowl. Add the black olives and capers to taste. Toss with just enough vinaigrette to moisten the lettuce – don't use too much. Place the cheeses under grill or in very hot oven, until they are beginning to brown on top and ooze tantalisingly. Remove the cheeses, arrange on the salad bowl and serve. Salads can be served in individual dishes, each topped with a goat's cheese.

Van Styvesant koolslaa

This salad was brought to New York by the Dutch settlers in 1624.

Ingredients   Serves six

500 g (16 oz) finely shredded white cabbage
4 tablespoons light malt vinegar (or any mild vinegar)
1 tablespoon sugar
¼ teaspoon black pepper
1 teaspoon Dijon mustard
1 tablespoon butter
1 egg
2 tablespoons double cream

Method

Place the cabbage in a bowl. In a separate bowl, lightly beat egg. Heat the vinegar, sugar, pepper, mustard and butter in a saucepan over a low heat, until boiling. Add some of the hot mixture to the egg, mix well then stir back into the vinegar mixture. Cook stirring until the mixture thickens and boils. Remove from the heat. Stir in the cream and pour while still hot, over the cabbage. Toss. Chill and serve cold.

Onion salad

Ingredients   **Serves two to three**

  1 small red onion
  1 small Spanish onion
  1 red pepper
  4 spring onions
  16 pitted Spanish olives
  2 tablespoons wine vinegar
  ¼ cup extra virgin olive oil
  2 teaspoons anchovy paste
  freshly ground black pepper

Method
Peel and cut the onions and pepper into slices and place in a serving bowl. Peel and dice the spring onions. Chill. Place the vinegar, oil and anchovy paste in a bowl and beat vigorously. Drain the olives and arrange on the salad. Pour the dressing over, sprinkle with pepper. Serve.

Chicken almond salad

Ingredients   **Serves four**

  350 g (12 oz) diced cooked chicken
  175 g (6 oz) raisins
  50 g (2 oz) blanched almonds
  2 tablespoons chopped parsley
  3 tablespoons diced spring onions
  1 tablespoon lemon juice
  2 tablespoons Hellman's real (or any starch-free) mayonnaise
  ¼ pint single cream
  lettuce leaves

Method
Soften the raisins in a little cold water, bring to the boil and stand for 5 minutes. Strain and cool. Combine with the chicken,

almonds, parsley and spring onion. Mix the lemon juice into the mayonnaise and add the cream. Pour over the chicken mixture and toss to blend. Place spoonfuls on lettuce leaves and serve.

Salad niçoise

Ingredients   **Serves four**
  6 or 8 lettuce leaves from the heart of a crisp iceberg lettuce
  6 ripe medium-sized tomatoes
  3 hard-boiled eggs
  500 g (1 lb) can tuna
  6 anchovy fillets
  16 black olives
  4 tablespoons virgin olive oil
  1 tablespoon wine vinegar
  1 clove garlic
  2 tablespoons chopped fresh parsley
  1 teaspoon capers
  salt and freshly ground black pepper

Method
Place the lettuce leaves whole in a bowl, unless they are very large, in which case tear them in half. Cut the tomatoes and eggs into quarters. Roughly flake the tuna. Add all to the lettuce leaves.

Peel the garlic and crush with the blade of a heavy knife, sprinkling salt on the garlic and crushing several times. Rinse the capers. Pour the olive oil and vinegar into a screw-top jar. Add the garlic, capers, parsley and ground pepper. Shake until blended. Pour over the salad and toss lightly. Place in individual dishes, scatter the olives over and lay the anchovy fillets on top.

Roast beef and asparagus salad

Ingredients   **Serves two to three**
  225 g (8 oz) leftover rare roast beef
  225 g (8 oz) cooked, cold, fresh asparagus (not canned)
  2 small (200 g) raw courgettes
  250 g punnet cherry tomatoes, halved
  1 or 2 little gem lettuces

Dressing
   4 *tablespoons plain yoghurt*
   1½ *tablespoons starch-free tomato ketchup*
   1 *teaspoon mild smooth Dijon mustard*

Method
Slice the beef into strips. Wash the lettuce leaves and leave whole.
Peel the courgettes and slice into long thin strips. Combine the
beef, asparagus, courgettes, tomatoes and lettuce. Combine the
dressing ingredients and pour over the salad before serving.

Watercress salad with egg dressing

Ingredients   **Serves four**
   3 *bunches watercress*
   4 *hard-boiled eggs*
   1½ *tablespoons wine vinegar*
   ¾ *teaspoon salt*
   freshly ground black pepper
   1 *tablespoon Dijon mustard*
   4 *tablespoons safflower oil*
   3 *tablespoons olive oil*
   2 *tablespoons non-starch mayonnaise*

Method
Wash and dry the watercress and remove the heavy stems.
Place in a large bowl. Finely chop the eggs. In a screw-top jar,
combine the vinegar, salt, pepper, mustard and oils. Shake to
combine. Pour into a small bowl, then add the mayonnaise and
half the chopped eggs. Blend and pour enough of this mixture
over the watercress to coat well. Toss. Sprinkle the remaining
eggs over. Serve.

Tanya's courgette salad

Ingredients   **Serves two to three**
   500 g (1 lb) *young courgettes*
   2 *tablespoons olive oil*
   salt and pepper
   5–6 *tablespoons Greek yoghurt*
   2 *tablespoons roughly chopped basil leaves*

Method

Wash and grate the courgettes, unpeeled. Heat the oil in a frying pan and add the courgettes. Sprinkle with salt and pepper and toss in the oil until just warmed through. Mix the basil into the yoghurt. Place the courgettes in a serving dish and pour the yoghurt over.

Aussie red heart salad

Ingredients   **Serves eight**
   ½ *red cabbage, sliced finely*
   1 packet best-quality dried apricots
   6 spring onions
   salt and freshly ground black pepper
   450 ml (16 fl oz) virgin olive oil
   1 clove garlic
   150 ml (¼ pint) balsamic vinegar
   1 teaspoon Dijon peppercorn mustard

Method

Place the cabbage in a shallow salad bowl and arrange the apricots on top. Chop the spring onions and scatter over. Lightly season with salt and pepper. Peel the garlic and crush with the blade of a knife, sprinkling with salt. Combine all the dressing ingredients in a screw-top jar, add the garlic and shake well. Pour the dressing over the salad and allow it to stand for about 30 minutes. Toss just before serving.

Unbelievably simple salad

Ingredients
   2 large or 3 medium sweet tomatoes per person
   2 teaspoons chopped chives per person
   2 tablespoons double cream per person
   salt and freshly ground black pepper

Method

Wash the tomatoes and slice thinly. Place on a large serving plate. Add the chopped chives to the double cream, season with the salt and a grind of pepper and spoon over the tomatoes.

Greek salad

In Greece they call this the 'village salad' – *choriátiki saláta*.

Ingredients   **Serves six**
  3 large firm tomatoes
  1 large cucumber
  1 medium onion
  2 green peppers
  1 cup black olives
  200 g (8 oz) feta cheese
  handful each of finely chopped basil and parsley
  100 ml (4 fl oz) virgin olive oil
  4 tablespoons malt vinegar
  1 clove garlic, crushed
  salt and black pepper

Method
Cut the tomatoes into chunks, slice the onions and green
peppers. Peel the cucumber if the skin is tough, otherwise slice
or cube. Place in a salad bowl and lightly sprinkle with salt and
freshly ground black pepper. Toss gently. Cube the feta cheese
and add to the bowl with the olives and herbs. Peel and crush
the garlic with the blade of a knife, sprinkling with salt and
crushing several times. Pour the oil and vinegar into a screw-
top jar, add the garlic, shake vigorously and pour over the salad.
Toss gently again and serve.

Spinach, anchovy and egg salad

Ingredients   **Serves four**
  enough raw spinach for four
  4 hard-boiled eggs
  8 anchovy fillets
  4 tablespoons of your favourite dressing or this recipe:
    6 tablespoons virgin olive oil
    2 tablespoons white wine vinegar
    1 clove garlic

Method
Wash the spinach thoroughly, remove the stems, shake dry and
drain in a colander. If the leaves are large, break them into bite-

sized pieces and arrange in a salad bowl. Drain the anchovy fillets on a paper towel, cut into quarters and add to the spinach.

Make a dressing by blending the oil and wine in a screw-top jar. Peel and crush the garlic sprinkled in salt with the blade of a knife, then add to the jar and shake vigorously.

Cut two of the eggs into quarters and chop the other two finely. Just before serving, pour the dressing over the spinach and toss. Sprinkle the chopped eggs over and arrange the quartered eggs around the edge of the bowl.

Spinach and bacon with blue cheese dressing

Ingredients   Serves four
   80 g (2–3) streaky bacon rashers
   enough raw spinach for four
   3 hard-boiled eggs
   bunch of chives
   225 g (8 oz) sweet cherry tomatoes

Dressing
   1 tablespoon sugar
   1 teaspoon salt
   1 teaspoon Dijon mustard
   freshly ground black pepper
   3 tablespoons wine vinegar
   150 ml (¼ pint) salad oil
   125 g (4 oz) Roquefort or Danish blue cheese

Method
Dice the bacon and cook over a very low heat until crisp – don't let it burn. Drain. Wash the spinach well, drain and if the leaves are large, tear them into bite-sized pieces. Put in a salad bowl. Wash the tomatoes, chop the chives and add to the salad with the bacon. Toss lightly. Chop the eggs finely and scatter over the salad.

Combine all the dressing ingredients, except the cheese, in a screw-top jar and shake until blended. In a separate bowl, mash the cheese and add enough dressing to make it sufficiently pourable (about half a cup). Pour over the salad and toss lightly. Left-over dressing can be used in other salads.

Tomato and anchovy salad

Ingredients   **Serves four**
6–8 medium sweet tomatoes
2 teaspoons salt
1 bunch chives
6 fresh basil leaves
45 g (2 oz) tin anchovies in oil

Dressing
freshly ground black pepper
150 ml (¼ pint) virgin olive oil
4 cloves garlic
3 tablespoons white wine vinegar or sherry vinegar
pinch sugar
salt and freshly ground black pepper

Method
Make the vinaigrette first: peel the garlic, sprinkle with salt and crush under the blade of a strong knife. Sprinkle with salt and crush several times. Combine the oil and vinegar in a screw-top jar, add the garlic, sugar and pepper. Shake vigorously and allow to stand for several hours.

Place the tomatoes in a bowl and pour boiling water over them. After a few seconds spear each one with a fork and peel off the skin. Slice the tomatoes thickly, place in a colander and sprinkle with salt. Leave to drain for about an hour. Blot dry and arrange on a serving dish.

Chop the herbs, open the tin of anchovies and drain. Spoon the vinaigrette over the tomatoes, sprinkle the herbs over and lay anchovies in a lattice pattern on top. Grind with pepper and serve.

Salmon salad

This salad can be a complete meal for two or a complete meal for one and a side-salad for one, depending on what you want.

Ingredients   **Serves one or two**
   1 or 2 little gem lettuces
   3 sticks celery
   1 large firm tomato
   ½ red pepper
   ½ yellow pepper
   1 tablespoon chopped parsley
   213 g (8 oz) can pink salmon
   vinaigrette dressing of your choice

Method
Wash all the vegetables. Separate the leaves of the lettuce, break into bite-sized pieces and put in a serving bowl. Chop the celery, slice the red and yellow peppers into strips, cut the tomato into segments, chop the parsley and add them all to the lettuce. Pour a little dressing over the vegetables and toss. Add the salmon and toss lightly again. Serve.

Peppered chicken salad

Ingredients   **Serves two**
   A variety of greens such as: 2 leaves iceberg lettuce, 2 leaves lollo
      rosso, 2 little gem lettuces or 4–5 leaves cos lettuce
   handful rocket leaves
   handful spinach
   tablespoon chopped chives
   tablespoon chopped parsley
   6 sliced mushrooms
   about a dozen whole cherry tomatoes
   2 cold breasts of peppered chicken cooked in foil (see page 106)

Method
Wash and break the lettuce leaves into bite-sized pieces and place in a salad bowl. Wash the tomatoes, chop the herbs and mushrooms, and add to the bowl. Chop the chicken into strips or cubes, add to the bowl and pour your favourite vinaigrette dressing over, or use your own mayonnaise.

Cucumber salad Damascus

Cool and refreshing. Try this with rich meat dishes.

Ingredients   **Serves two**
    1 cucumber
    2 tablespoons plain yoghurt
    ½ clove garlic
    2 tablespoons chopped chives
    1 tablespoon chopped mint
    salt and pepper to taste

Method
Peel the cucumbers, slice thinly and place in a mixing bowl.
Peel and crush the garlic, chop the chives and mint and add to
the yoghurt. Season to taste. Pour over the cucumbers and toss
together.

American salad

The Americans love salads made with fruit. They often serve
them before the main course, but this is a wonderful summer
salad served with ham or gammon.

Ingredients   **Serves two to three**
    whole lettuce leaves
    2 fresh peaches
    4 halved canned pears
    20 fresh cherries
    1 small or ½ large cucumber
    4 tablespoons vinaigrette

Method
Peel the cucumber and slice thinly. Slice the pears, peel the
peaches and slice by cutting into the stone all around the peach
until the segments fall off (like a chocolate orange). Cut the cherries in half and remove pits. Combine all in a salad bowl, then toss
in the vinaigrette. Serve in lettuce 'cups' on individual plates.

American 'jello' salads

The first time I was invited to dinner with American friends and saw fruit salad in jelly on the table, I assumed it was for dessert. To my surprise, it was part of the main course. I discovered it is delicious with meat – and why not? After all, we enjoy red-currant or mint jelly with lamb – a 'jello' salad is just a more imaginative version. The fruit used can be fresh or canned and should be well-drained. A tablespoon of lemon juice or any mild vinegar can be added if desired. Leftover juice can be added to the liquid required for the jelly. Fresh, uncooked pineapple and kiwi fruit will prevent the jelly from setting. Canned pineapple is fine, but kiwi fruit is best used only as a garnish. Here are two versions.

Version 1 ingredients
1 lime jelly
about 250 g (12 oz) sliced pears, apricots and sweet green grapes

Version 2 ingredients
1 orange jelly
about 250 g (12 oz) orange segments and strawberries

Method
Make the jelly according to the directions, then add the fruit. Set either in a jelly mould, individual moulds or an ordinary deep dish. Brush the mould with light salad oil before pouring the liquid jelly in. Chill until firm. Unmould and serve on a bed of lettuce or garnished with watercress or parsley.

Warm garlic tomato salad

Ingredients
1 box sweet cherry tomatoes
75 g (3 oz) butter
1 teaspoon garlic granules
salt and freshly ground black pepper

Method
Melt the butter in a frying pan over a low heat. Add the garlic granules and heat but do not brown. Add the tomatoes. Heat for 4 minutes over a very low heat, sprinkle with salt and pepper to taste. Serve hot on a bed of lettuce or watercress.

Puddings and desserts

Most of the recipes in this section and in the baking section use fruit sugar. If you find ordinary sugar causes no IBS symptoms for you, you can use granulated, castor or brown sugar instead.

Spiced apricot compote

This is best made in a slow cooker, the bottom oven of an Aga or in an ordinary oven on very low heat 85°C (180°F) for 8 hours or overnight. If you have a gas cooker, use the lowest setting ($\frac{1}{4}$ or $\frac{1}{2}$ or S) and put the dish on the base plate, overnight. It can also be cooked for 4 hours in a moderate oven at 170°C (325°F, gas mark 3). It is wonderful served with plain Greek yoghurt or vanilla ice-cream.

Ingredients   **Serves four to six**
  275 g (10 oz) dried apricots
  150 ml ($\frac{1}{4}$ pint) sweet white wine or sherry
  450 ml (3/4 pint) water
  25 g (1 oz) fruit sugar
  2 tablespoons mild flavoured honey
  1 large orange, finely grated zest and juice
  1 teaspoon whole cloves

Method
Put the apricots in a flame-proof casserole, pour in the wine and water, then stir in the sugar and honey. Heat gently until dissolved, then bring to the boil. Remove from the heat, add the orange zest and juice and the cloves. Cover the casserole and cook slowly as above. Cool and remove the cloves before serving.

Brandied prune mousse

Ingredients   **Serves six**
  225 g (8 oz) pitted prunes
  water to cover prunes
  2 tablespoons fruit sugar
  4 tablespoons reserved prune liquid
  2 egg whites from size 1 eggs
  100 ml (4 fl oz) double cream
  1 tablespoon brandy

Method

Cover the prunes with water and soak overnight. Bring to the boil, add the sugar and simmer for 15 minutes. Drain, reserving liquid and allow to cool. Purée the prunes in a liquidiser with 4 tablespoons of the reserved liquid or push through a sieve and add the liquid. Place in a large basin. Stir in the brandy. In a smaller basin whip the egg whites until stiff. Whip the cream separately. Fold the cream into the prune mixture and gently fold in the egg whites. Place in a serving dish and chill.

Creamy lemon freeze

Ingredients   **Serves six**

125 g (4 oz) ground almonds
75 g (3 oz) butter
1–2 tablespoons fruit sugar
2 separated size 2 eggs
397 g full-cream sweetened condensed milk
85 ml (3 fl oz) lemon juice
½ teaspoon grated lemon zest
3 tablespoons caster sugar

Method

Melt the butter over a low heat. Add the ground almonds and cook gently until they begin to brown. Remove from the heat, stir in the fruit sugar to combine well and press into an oblong plastic food box, or loaf tin and place in the freezer.

Beat the egg yolks until thick. Combine with the condensed milk, juice and peel. Beat the egg whites with caster sugar into a stiff meringue. Fold into the lemon mixture.

Remove the ground almonds from the freezer, pour the lemon mixture over the almond base and freeze.

Apple soufflé

Ingredients

2 large bramley apples or 450 g (1 lb) apple purée
100 g (4 oz) caster sugar
3 size 2 eggs
150 ml (¼ pint) crème fraîche
1 tablespoon Calvados

Method

If using fresh apples, peel, slice and cook them in a little water until soft enough to give a thick purée. Separate the eggs, whisk the whites until stiff and set them aside. Beat the yolks, sugar, Calvados and crème fraîche until thick and add the apple. Blend well. Fold in the egg whites and pour into a greased soufflé dish and bake in preheated oven (180°C, 350°F, gas mark 4) for 50–60 minutes or until just set. Serve hot or warm with cream.

Choc-orange mousse

Easy to make with a blender or food processor.

Ingredients   **Serves eight**

300 ml (½ pint) *double cream*
200 g (7 oz) *plain (dark) chocolate*
2 tablespoons *fruit sugar*
4 egg yolks
1 tablespoon *Grand Marnier*
1 teaspoon *vanilla*
2 teaspoons *grated orange zest*
50 g (2 oz) *unsalted butter*

Optional topping

1 *whole orange*
200 ml (7 fl oz) *water*
100 g (4 oz) *fruit or granulated sugar*
125 ml (4 fl oz) *double or whipping cream*
2 teaspoons *Grand Marnier*

Method

Break or chop the chocolate and place it, with the butter, in the top of a double boiler or in a bowl set into a saucepan, a quarter filled with water (do not let the bowl touch the bottom). Melt together over simmering water. Add 300 ml cream to the chocolate mixture and heat slowly, stirring, until bubbles form around edges (do not boil) then remove from the heat.

Meanwhile, grate the orange zest and place in a food blender with the egg yolks, sugar and Grand Marnier. Begin to blend the egg mixture on low speed while pouring in the hot chocolate/cream mixture, then blend all together on high speed for about a minute or until smooth. Pour into 8 small serving glasses, refrigerate 1 to 2 hours before serving. Serve with whipped cream or topping.

For the topping, peel the rind thinly from the orange or use a zester, and boil for 5 minutes in plain water. Drain and cut into thread-like strips. Combine the water and sugar, bring to the boil, add the orange rind and cook until rind is transparent (about 4 minutes). Remove and cool. Beat the cream and Grand Marnier until thick. Pipe or blob spoonfuls of cream on the serving dishes with the orange rind twirled on top.

Superb cheesecake

Most shop-bought cheesecakes include cornflour or flour, but there's no need. This is an absolutely brilliant recipe – however, a word of warning about cream cheese. I have discovered that the Philadelphia brand, when tested with iodine, goes a strange olive-greenish colour, indicating there may be starchy additions not listed on the pack. Plain unbranded cream cheese from the deli counter of your supermarket or food store is fine.

Ingredients   **Serves eight**

700 g (1 lb 7 oz) unbranded cream cheese – not low-fat
75 g (3 oz) caster sugar
125 g (4½ oz) mild-flavoured honey
5 large eggs
100 ml (4 fl oz) thick sour cream
100 ml (4 fl oz) double cream
1½ teaspoons freshly grated lemon zest
75 ml (2½ fl oz) lemon juice
½ teaspoon salt

Method
Prepare a 24 cm (9½ inch) diameter round spring-form cake tin by buttering all over the sides and bottom and sprinkling with icing sugar (make sure the icing sugar is starch-free). Shake upside-down over the sink to remove surplus sugar. Or, alternatively, line an ordinary cake tin with baking parchment – cut a circle for the bottom and strips for the side. If you wish, this can be made in a loaf tin or casserole dish, but whatever

you use, it must be properly prepared so that cheesecake can be turned out easily.

In a large bowl, beat the cream cheese with an electric beater until light and fluffy, adding the sugar and honey gradually, and beating until well combined. Add the eggs one at a time, then both creams, vanilla essence, lemon zest, juice and salt. Pour the mixture into the prepared tin and bake in a moderate oven (170°C–180°C, 350°F, gas mark 4) for 1 hour. Check the cake – if the top is getting too brown, lay a sheet of baking parchment or brown paper on top. If the cake springs back leaving no fingerprint when it is touched in the middle, it is ready. Turn off the oven, open the oven door and leave to cool.

Refrigerate overnight. Turn out onto a serving plate the next day. Serve with whole strawberries covered with strawberry sauce. This may require a longer cooking – I cooked it for 2 hours in a loaf tin.

Key lime mousse

One of the most popular desserts in America is key lime pie. Here is an adapted version – just as delicious without the pie crust. Key limes are an American variety unobtainable here, so this is not really key lime anything, but the name is so famous and so often heard being ordered in restaurants with guilty greed, that I couldn't resist using it. Ordinary limes will do just as well.

Ingredients   **Serves four to six**
   1 envelope unflavoured gelatine
   100 ml (4 fl oz) fresh lime juice
   125 g (4½ oz) fruit sugar
   125 g (4½ oz) mild-flavoured honey
   2 large eggs, beaten
   175 g (6 oz) natural full-cream cream cheese (unbranded)
   175 g (6 oz) butter, softened
   500 ml (18 fl oz) whipping cream, divided
   1½ teaspoons grated lime zest

Method
Wash the limes, grate the zest and set aside. Squeeze the juice and pour it into a medium-sized saucepan. Sprinkle the

gelatine over the juice and allow to stand for 5 minutes. Beat the eggs and add with the sugar and honey to the juice. Stir with a wooden spoon or wire whisk until blended. Cook over a medium heat, stirring constantly, until the mixture comes to the boil. Reduce the heat and simmer, stirring constantly, for about 3 minutes or until thickened. Remove from the heat and set aside.

Beat the cream cheese and butter with an electric beater until smooth. Gradually add the lime juice mixture, beating well. Cover and chill for 25 minutes, stirring occasionally.

Beat 250 ml (9 fl oz) of whipping cream until stiff peaks form. Fold into the chilled lime mixture. Cover and chill for a further 25 minutes, stirring occasionally.

Beat the remaining cream until stiff peaks form. Fold into the chilled mixture with the grated zest. Pour into individual dishes if desired. Cover and chill for 4 hours or until firm.

Strawberry and yoghurt sorbet

Ingredients   **Serves four**
   125 g (4½ oz) fruit sugar
   150 ml (¼ pint) water
   250 g (9 oz) strawberries
   225 ml (8 fl oz) plain mild low-fat yoghurt
   1 egg white

Method
Combine the sugar and water in a saucepan, stir constantly over heat without boiling until the sugar is dissolved. Bring to the boil, reduce the heat, simmer uncovered without stirring for five minutes or until the mixture is thick. Cool the sugar syrup to room temperature and refrigerate until cold.

Blend or process the strawberries and yoghurt until smooth, add the sugar syrup and blend. Pour mixture into a pie dish or oblong plastic food container or similar, cover with foil and freeze for several hours or until set.

Beat the egg white until stiff, remove the frozen mixture, break it up with a fork, beat until smooth and fold in the egg white. Return to the container and freeze again until set. This can be made three days ahead and kept covered in the freezer.

Brandied figs

Ingredients   Serves three
   12 fresh figs
   225 ml (8 fl oz) brandy
   75 g (3 oz) fruit sugar
   125 g (4½ oz) honey
   double cream or Greek yoghurt

Method
Peel the figs and place in a bowl. Dissolve the sugar and honey
in the brandy, pour over the figs and chill in the refrigerator for
several hours or overnight. Turn the figs occasionally to make
sure all are well soaked in the brandy. Serve with double cream
or Greek yoghurt.

Baked apple slices

Ingredients   Serves 2
   500 g (1 lb) bramley apples
   2 tablespoons fruit sugar
   about 30 g (1 oz) butter
   piece of lemon zest (optional)

Method
Peel, core and slice the apples and place in a single layer in a
shallow oven-proof dish. Sprinkle the sugar over evenly, cut
the butter into small pieces and dot all over (you may need a
little more). Wash a lemon and carefully peel a slice off the skin
making sure you get only the zest and none of the bitter white
pith underneath. Place the peel in the centre of the dish and
cook, uncovered, and without any water, in the top of a
medium oven for about 30 minutes. Check that all the slices are
cooking evenly from time to time, and turn them over halfway
through the cooking. Delicious hot or cold, with ice cream,
custard or cream, or as the filling for a sweet puffy omelette.

In cider
Omit the lemon peel and butter. Pour in some cider up to two thirds the height of the apples and cook as above.

In orange juice
Use orange juice and grated orange peel instead of cider.

Sweet puffy omelette

Ingredients   Serves two to three
3 eggs
2 tablespoons caster sugar
either a sherry glass of any sweet liqueur such as Grand Marnier,
    Cointreau, Kirsch, cherry brandy, apricot brandy or rum
    (optional) or 3 tablespoons of milk or cream
25 g (1 oz) butter

Method
Preheat the oven to a moderate heat (180°C, 350°F, gas mark 4). Separate the eggs into two medium-sized mixing bowls. Add 1 tablespoon of sugar to the whites and beat until stiff. Add 1 tablespoon of sugar to the yolks and beat until thick and lemon-coloured. Beat in the liqueur or cream or milk. Fold the white mixture carefully into the yolks.

Melt the butter over a high heat in a heavy frying pan with an oven-proof handle. When the butter is sizzling, pour the egg mixture in and turn the heat to low. Cook slowly until light brown underneath (about 10 minutes). Bubbles will still appear through the uncooked puffy top and the mixture will look moist. Remove the frying pan and place in the oven. Bake until the omelette is light brown on top and springs back leaving no fingerprint when lightly touched in middle (about 10–15 minutes). Remove from the oven, make a deep crease across the omelette, place any filling on one half, slip a spatula underneath to loosen, fold over and turn out onto a warm plate. Slice into wedges and serve with cream. This is wonderful with strawberries marinated in orange juice, or raspberry purée.

Low-cal baked apple

Ingredients　　　　　　　　　　　　　　　　　　**Serves one**
   handful sultanas or raisins
   1 teaspoon runny honey
   4 tablespoons unsweetened orange juice
   1 large eating apple

Method
Put the dried fruit, honey and orange juice in a basin and stand
for at least 10 minutes. Wash the apple well, core but do not
peel, and stand in an oven-proof dish. Spoon the dried fruit into
the hole, pour the juice over, cover with a lid or foil and bake
in slow–moderate oven (170°C, 325°F, gas mark 3) for 45
minutes.

Custard sauce

We can't eat ordinary custard made with custard powder, or
any bought custard, whether in packs or cans, on trifles or
mixed with fruit or jelly. But we can eat proper custard made
with eggs, which is much more delicious.

Custard sauce can be made in an ordinary heavy-based
saucepan if you are an experienced cook and you stir constantly with a wooden spoon to prevent the mixture from
curdling. Even if curdling does occur, a lump of butter stirred
in at the end will make the mixture smooth again. But all good
cooks say (and I agree) that it is best made in a double boiler or
a bowl fitted into a saucepan of simmering water (don't let the
bottom of the bowl rest on the bottom of the saucepan). Well-
made egg custard sauce is one of the great dishes of the world.
Here is the recommended standard version.

Ingredients　　　　　　　　　　　　　　　　　　**Serves four**
   4 egg yolks or 2 whole eggs
   30 g (1 oz) fruit sugar
   ¼ teaspoon salt
   350 ml (12 fl oz) milk
   1 teaspoon vanilla essence

Method

Quarter fill a saucepan or the bottom of double boiler with water and stand over the heat to boil. Whisk the sugar, salt and eggs together until the mixture is thick and almost white. Bring the milk almost to the boil and pour through a sieve into the egg mixture, stirring at the same time. Reduce the heat under the water until it is simmering. Place the bowl (or top of double boiler) containing the egg mixture over simmering water and stir constantly. As soon as the mixture begins to coat the spoon and before it begins to boil, remove from the heat, add the vanilla and continue stirring for a couple of minutes.

Floating island custard

Ingredients   Serves four
   2 egg whites
   $\frac{1}{4}$ teaspoon salt
   2 tablespoons caster sugar
   750 ml (1$\frac{1}{2}$ pints) milk

Custard sauce
   3 whole eggs
   2 egg yolks
   3 tablespoons fruit sugar
   pinch salt
   1$\frac{1}{2}$ teaspoons vanilla essence
   more milk if needed

Method

Beat egg whites with salt and sugar until stiff. In large diameter saucepan or deep frying pan, bring the milk to simmer and drop rounded tablespoonfuls of egg white mixture on top. Poach gently, uncovered, in the simmering milk until firm (about 5 minutes). Remove the meringues with a spatula and set aside on a plate.

Beat whole eggs, egg yolks, sugar and salt together until thick. Measure the heated milk and add more to make up to 750 ml (1$\frac{1}{2}$ pints) if necessary. Pour through a sieve onto the egg mixture and place in the top of a double boiler or in a bowl in a saucepan and cook, stirring constantly, as in the standard custard recipe. Remove from the heat, add the vanilla and continue to stir for a while. Pour into a serving bowl. Place the meringues on top. Chill and serve.

Crème anglaise

This is the deluxe version of custard sauce as made by the French and named after the English – who usually only make the standard version.

Ingredients   **Serves four**
  1 vanilla pod
  500 ml (18 fl oz) milk
  8 size 3 egg yolks
  75 g (3 oz) fruit sugar
  pinch salt

Method
Split the vanilla pod in half lengthways and place in the milk. Bring to the boil and remove from the heat. Leave to infuse for 15 minutes. Whisk sugar, salt and egg yolks until the mixture is almost white. Return the milk to the heat and almost bring to the boil, pour through a sieve into the egg mixture stirring constantly, and cook in a double boiler or a bowl over simmering water as in the standard recipe – but do not add any extra vanilla at the end. Additional flavours such as Kirsch, rum or brandy can be stirred into the cooled custard.

Baked custard

Ingredients   **Serves two to three**
  3 eggs
  450 ml (16 fl oz) milk
  25 g (1 oz) fruit sugar
  pinch salt
  1 teaspoon vanilla essence

Method
Bring the milk almost to the boil, remove from the heat. Whisk the eggs, sugar and salt together until combined and pour the milk over, continuing to whisk. Add the vanilla essence and pour into a pie dish and stand this in a large pan of hot water

shallow enough to come halfway up the side of the pie dish. Place in slow oven (150°C, 300°F, gas mark 2) and bake for an hour or until a knife inserted in the custard, slightly off-centre, comes out clean. Remove and serve warm or chilled.

Crème caramel

Ingredients   **Serves six**
   5 tablespoons fruit sugar
   150 ml (¼ pint) water
   7 eggs
   775 ml (1½ pints) milk
   100 ml (4 fl oz) double cream
   1 teaspoon vanilla essence
   4 tablespoons fruit sugar
   pinch salt

Method
In a small saucepan over a low heat, dissolve the sugar in the water, stirring constantly. When dissolved, stop stirring and allow it to boil rapidly until it turns golden brown. Remove from the heat and pour immediately into a deep, round oven-proof dish. Quickly tilt the dish to make the caramel coat the bottom of the dish evenly. Set aside.

Lightly whisk the eggs, sugar and salt together in a bowl. Heat the milk and cream to just under boiling, then pour this over the egg mixture, whisking continuously. Add the vanilla essence. Pour the mixture through a sieve onto the caramel mixture. Place in a large baking pan filled with enough hot water to come halfway up the side of the dish.

Bake in a slow oven (150C, 300°F, gas mark 2) for 40 minutes to an hour, or until a knife inserted in centre comes out clean. Remove and cool to room temperature before chilling overnight.

To serve, run a knife around the inside edge to loosen, put a serving dish over the top and turn upside-down.

Crème brûlée

Some people may find the gilled sugar may cause mild IBS symptoms. Grilled fruit sugar will brown very rapidly, so take care.

Ingredients   **Serves six**
   6 egg yolks
   4 tablespoons brown sugar or fruit sugar
   500 ml (about 1 pint) whipping cream
   250 ml (about ½ pint) double cream
   pinch salt
   2 teaspoons vanilla essence
   further fruit sugar or brown sugar

Method
Beat the egg yolks, 4 tablespoons of fruit sugar and salt together until thick. Heat the cream in the top of a double boiler or a bowl set in a saucepan of simmering water until nearly boiling. Remove and pour over the eggs, stirring continuously. Stir in the vanilla and pour all through a sieve into an oven-proof dish set in a baking pan of hot water. Bake 1–1½ hours in a moderate oven (160°C, 300°F, gas mark 2) until a knife inserted into the centre comes out clean. Do not overbake – the custard will continue to cook from retained heat when it is removed from the oven. Cool and chill overnight. Before serving, cover the entire surface with fruit sugar or brown sugar, set in a dish of cracked ice and put under the grill until the sugar melts and browns.

Peach clafouti

Ingredients   **Serves 2**
   325 g can peach slices
   750 g (1½ lb) Ricotta cheese
   2 teaspoons grated lemon zest
   2 tablespoons peach juice
   75 g (3 oz) fruit sugar
   100 ml (4 fl oz) full-cream evaporated milk
   2 eggs

Method
Drain the peaches, saving the juice, and lay the slices on the bottom of a deep oven-proof dish. Wash the lemon carefully and grate the zest. Beat the Ricotta cheese with an electric beater until fluffy. Beat in the milk, rind, peach juice, sugar and eggs. Pour over the peach slices and bake in a moderate oven at

180°C (350°F or gas mark 4) for about 50 minutes or until a knife inserted into the centre comes out clean.

This recipe can also be made with baked apple slices (see page 166).

Swiss cream

Ingredients   **Serves four**
  1 jelly – any flavour
  1 cup boiling water
  410 g (large can) full-cream evaporated milk

Method
Chill the can of milk overnight or put it in the freezer for $1\frac{1}{2}$ hours. Make up the jelly with the boiling water, according to instructions. Leave until cool. Pour the chilled milk into a large bowl and beat with an electric beater until thick. Pour the cooled jelly into the milk and beat again. Leave to set.

Wine jelly

Ingredients   **Serves three to four**
  1 raspberry jelly
  225 ml (8 fl oz) boiling water
  225 ml (8 fl oz) red wine

Method
Make up the jelly according to the instructions with the boiling water. Cool. Add the wine. Pour into small serving dishes and chill. Serve with cream and summer fruits.

Orange yoghurt with raspberries

Ingredients   **Serves six**
  500 g (1 lb) carton of mild low-fat plain or Greek yoghurt
  $\frac{1}{2}$ jar of orange curd – see recipe using fruit sugar on page 214 (If
    made from bought curd, make sure it is starch-free)
  1 carton frozen raspberries
  2 tablespoons fruit sugar
  2 teaspoons water (optional)

Method
Put the raspberries (either frozen or defrosted) in a small saucepan and bring slowly to the boil. You do not need to add any water unless you prefer a less intense taste – you can always add it afterwards if you think it is needed. Stir gently so as not to break up the fruit and when simmering remove from the heat. Add fruit sugar to taste, gently mixing until it is dissolved. Chill.

Pour the yoghurt into a mixing bowl and blend with the orange curd. Use more curd if wished. Chill. Serve the raspberries in small glass bowls topped with the yoghurt.

Perfect pavlova

This is an unconventional method that really works. It makes a perfect crisp crust with soft marshmallow centre – and it does not drop when you take it out of the oven. Because it is cooked at such a low heat, it does not cause IBS symptoms unless you eat too much.

Ingredients
> 4 egg whites
> pinch salt
> 8 oz castor sugar
> 1 teaspoon each of vanilla essence and white vinegar
> 4 tablespoons boiling water

Method
Heat the oven to 200°C or 400°F or gas mark 6. Cut a piece of baking parchment or foil large enough to cover an oven tray. Butter well (rub all over with a lump of butter held in butter paper) and sprinkle with water.

Beat all the ingredients together with an electric mixer until it holds firm peaks when you take the beaters out of the mixture. Pile the mixture onto the prepared paper. The mixture will spread a little so make it into a rounded shape that is higher than you want the finished pavlova to be. Do not shape it with a hollow in the middle – this is not a true Pavlova. Place in the oven, close the door and turn the oven off. Leave for 1½ hours or overnight. To serve, cover with cream and decorate with fruit.

To make in an Aga, put the pavlova into the roasting oven for 7 minutes. Remove to the simmering oven for $4\frac{1}{2}$ hours.

A note of caution: in New Zealand, where I come from, it is traditional to decorate pavlovas with passionfruit or a passion-fruit sauce. Unfortunately, this is one of the few fruits which contains starch (in the pips) and this is especially intense when the fruit has been cooked. So do not use passionfruit.

Baking

Marie Antoinette's advice was right, 'If they can't eat bread, let them eat cake!' We can't eat bread – this is one food for which I cannot find a substitute. But I can offer some very good cakes and biscuits made without flour or starch.

Some 10 years ago when I first began experimenting with this diet, I missed cakes and pastries terribly. Now I no longer miss the comfort of these foods – I can pass even the most delicious cakes and biscuits without a second glance – but I would miss the convenience. Life is so much easier when you can snack on a biscuit or a piece of cake to keep you going.

I discovered there's virtually no such thing as a bought cake that is starch-free, so I was forced to devise my own recipes. A number of classic cakes are made with ground almonds which are quite a good substitute for the taste and texture of flour. The only trouble is that ground almonds are more expensive, make a far richer cake and one can't eat as much. However, they're very delicious and will help you feel less deprived.

If you've never done much baking before, I suggest you buy a good basic book with illustrations which show you how to prepare cake tins, test for 'doneness' – all the basic things that are not always spelled out in recipes. Baking is really rewarding and the secret is to be well organised. Read the recipe thoroughly, prepare the cake tins first and then assemble everything you need before you start mixing (as they do on TV cooking programmes).

You'll find baking parchment a great boon as you won't be able to butter and flour the cake tins. But there's a trick to using baking parchment successfully – butter or grease the tin you're going to cook in, *before* you line it with parchment, and the parchment will stick to the surface of the tin instead of slipping and sliding about.

My baking recipes usually include fruit sugar instead of ordinary sugar, but you can use ordinary sugar if you wish. Fruit sugar is slightly sweeter than ordinary sugar, so you may need to add an ounce or so extra when using ordinary sugar. The secret is to taste the mixture and see if it is sweet enough. The other characteristic of fruit sugar is that it allows the flavours of the other ingredients to come through more strongly. Chocolate is more chocolately – fruit is fruitier. You'll discover a whole new range of intense flavours.

Because oven temperatures tend to vary slightly, it is wise to test the cake for doneness yourself, rather than sticking exactly to a specific cooking time. I use two methods:

(1) Insert a heavy darning needle or fine skewer into the centre. If it comes out clean, the cake is cooked. If it still looks sticky, the cake is not ready.
(2) This method is best for light cakes. Touch the top lightly with a finger. If the finger print disappears, the cake is done.

It is better to remove a cake when slightly under-baked as it will carry on cooking as it stands.

You will also notice that some of my recipes use cooking chocolate, which does contain ordinary sugar. I have found that the amount of sugar in the chocolate does not really cause any problems – providing you don't sit down and eat the whole cake by yourself!

I also use honey as a sweetener – the chapter on starch explains why.

I hope these starch-free cakes and biscuits will help with your withdrawal pangs.

Basic cake batter

Ingredients
75 g (3 oz) butter
75 g (3 oz) fruit sugar or 30 g (1 oz) fruit sugar and 2 tablespoons (50 g) liquid honey
¼ teaspoon salt
3 eggs, separated
175 g (6 oz) ground almonds
1 teaspoon desired flavouring essence (optional)
sultanas, cherries, etc. (optional)

Method
This cake is not light and fluffy and will not rise greatly. It has a consistency similar to gingerbread. Prepare a cake tin with baking parchment. Beat the egg white until stiff. Cream the butter, salt, sugar and/or honey, and add egg yolks. Beat until

thick and creamy. Add essence and any fruit or chocolate. Add the ground almonds. Pour into the cake tin and bake in a moderate oven (180°C, 350°F, gas mark 4) for about an hour. Test after 50 minutes by inserting a large darning needle or fine skewer into the centre of the cake. If it comes out clean, the cake is cooked.

Plain cake
add 1 teaspoon of vanilla essence

Almond cake
add 1 teaspoon of almond essence (the ground almonds by themselves do not give a very almondy flavour)

Cherry cake
add 125 g (4½ oz) chopped cherries and ½ teaspoon of almond essence

Sultana cake
add 150 g (6 oz) sultanas and ½ teaspoon of vanilla or rum essence

Orange cake
add grated peel of an orange and 1 teaspoon of orange essence

Basic biscuit batter

If you've ever made choux pastry, this method will be familiar to you. I cannot be absolutely precise about the amount of ground almonds because it depends a great deal on how finely they are ground. The finest are almost like flour and 'bind' better than those of a slightly coarser grind. The recipe is a successful way of making a biscuit-type batter with many uses for savoury or sweet biscuits, cheesecake and pie bases or a sort of crumbly, cakey topping for fruit puddings. Experiment with your own ideas.

Ingredients
90 ml (3½ fl oz) water
30 g (1 oz) butter
90 g (3–4 oz) ground almonds
2 eggs

Method

Simmer the water and butter together in a saucepan until the butter is completely melted. Remove from the heat and add the almonds – enough for the mixture to have a dense consistency. Beat in the eggs with a wooden spoon until the mixture is thick and smoothish. Cool and add any of the variations below, blend well and place the mixture in spoonfuls or balls on a baking tray which has been prepared with baking parchment or well buttered. The mixture spreads somewhat during cooking. Bake in a moderate oven (180°C, 350°F, gas mark 4) until beginning to brown.

For cheese biscuits

To the dry ground almonds add:
125 g (4 oz) grated cheese
1 teaspoon salt

Blend well and add to the water/butter mixture, before beating in the eggs. Place on a piece of baking parchment and roll into a long log. Wrap in the parchment and chill for 30 minutes. Remove from refrigerator, slice into rounds and bake as above.

As a savoury pie base

Make the basic batter and press into pie dish. Bake as above. Cheese may be added as for cheese straws.

Sweet cookies

Add to the water and butter mixture:
2 level tablespoons fruit sugar
1 teaspoon various flavouring essences (see below)
$\frac{1}{4}$ teaspoon salt
Add any of the following to the cooled egg and almond mixture:

Plain biscuits

1 teaspoon vanilla essence

Almond biscuits

1 teaspoon almond essence

Chocolate chip cookies

1 teaspoon vanilla essence
100 g (4 oz) grated plain chocolate

Cherry cookies
1 teaspoon almond essence
100 g (4 oz) of chopped glacé cherries

Sultana or raisin cookies
1 teaspoon rum essence
100 g (4 oz) sultanas or raisins

Valencia cookies
1 teaspoon orange essence
60 g (2 oz) chopped orange peel

Sweet pie base
Make as for sweet cookies, but omit the flavouring essence. Press the mixture into the base of the prepared pie or cake tin. Add the filling and bake. For uncooked fillings the base must be cooked first.

Rich chocolate cake

Ingredients
250 g (9 oz) plain chocolate
175 g (6 oz) butter or margarine
75 g (3 oz) fruit sugar or 30 g (1 oz) fruit sugar and 2 tablespoons
*   liquid honey*
200 g (8 oz) ground almonds
1 teaspoon vanilla essence
4 eggs, separated
pinch salt
5 tablespoons apricot conserve

Method
Line a 22 cm ($8\frac{1}{2}$ inch) round cake tin with baking parchment. Melt 175 g (6 oz) of the plain chocolate in a bowl set in a saucepan of simmering water. When melted, stand in a warm place.

Whisk the egg whites with a pinch of salt until stiff. Cream 125 g (4 oz) of the butter with the sugar and/or honey until light and fluffy. Add the egg yolks and continue beating until creamy. Stir in the melted chocolate, ground almonds, vanilla essence and blend well. Fold in the egg whites.

Pour into the tin and bake for 55–60 minutes in a moderate

oven (160°C–180°C, 325°F–350°F, gas mark 3–4) or until done. Remove from oven and leave for a few minutes. Turn onto a wire rack and cool.

To ice the cake, warm the apricot conserve slightly in a small saucepan over a low heat. Spread over the top of the cake and allow it to cool completely. Put the remaining chocolate and the butter in a bowl set into a saucepan of simmering water and melt together. Spread over the top of the cake, allowing the mixture to run down the sides. This cake may sink slightly when cooking, but any cracks in the surface will be covered by the apricot and chocolate topping.

Chocolate coffee cheesecake

Ingredients

> 1 rich chocolate cake (as above) without apricot and chocolate topping
> 1 tablespoon coffee liqueur (Tia Maria or Kahlua)
> 1 tablespoon milk
> 250 g (9 oz) unbranded cream cheese
> 80 g (3 oz) ordinary sugar
> 1 egg
> 3 teaspoons gelatine
> 2 tablespoons water
> 3 tablespoons coffee liqueur, extra
> 300 ml (10 fl oz) extra thick double cream
> 2 teaspoons cocoa
> 2 teaspoons icing sugar
> 75 g flaked almonds

Method

Slice the chocolate cake carefully into two rounds so that one layer is thicker than the other. Place the thickest layer on the bottom of a 22 cm (8½ inch) loose-bottomed cake tin which has been buttered and lined with baking parchment – a circle for the base and two strips around the side coming right up the tin. Reserve the other layer of cake for the top.

Brush the bottom layer with half the combined coffee liqueur and milk. Combine the cream cheese with the sugar and egg and beat until smooth.

Sprinkle gelatine over the 2 tablespoons of water in a small bowl. Set in a saucepan of simmering water and stir to dissolve. Add the extra coffee liqueur to the gelatine and blend with the cream cheese mixture. Blend in the double cream. Pour the mixture into the cake tin over the cake base. Place the remaining layer of cake on top, brush with remaining coffee liqueur and milk mixture and refrigerate for several hours or overnight until set.

Remove from the tin. Peel the baking parchment away from sides and base, and place on a serving dish. Toast the flaked almonds by baking in a moderate oven for 5 minutes or until golden brown. Cool. Press the toasted almonds all over the cheesecake sides. Mix the cocoa and icing sugar together, put in a sieve and sprinkle over the top of the cake.

Amaretti biscuits

Ingredients
125 g (4½ oz) coarse ground almonds
225 g (8½ oz) ordinary sugar
2 large egg whites
½ teaspoon vanilla essence
½ teaspoon almond essence
¼ teaspoon salt
blanched almonds for decorating

Method
Combine the ground almonds, sugar, unbeaten egg whites, salt, vanilla and almond essences in a bowl. Beat the mixture for about three minutes. Let it stand for five minutes.

Butter a baking tray, line with baking parchment and butter again. Spoon the mixture into a piping bag fitted with a 1 cm (½ inch) plain tube. Pipe in a circular motion from the centre, to make biscuits about 4 cm (1½ inches) in diameter (they can be smaller). Place a blanched almond or almond half on top of each biscuit. Bake in a slow to moderate oven (140°C–160°C, 290°F–325°F, gas mark 2–3) for 12–15 minutes, until lightly browned. Leave on the tray for a few minutes before removing with a spatula to cool on a wire rack.

Florentines

Ingredients
125 g (4 oz) flaked almonds
30 g (1 oz) mixed peel
30 g (1 oz) glacé cherries – red and dark if possible
1 tablespoon sultanas
12 g (½ oz) angelica
12 g (½ oz) glacé pineapple
4 good-quality dried apricots
75 g (3 oz) butter
3 tablespoons fruit sugar or 1 tablespoon fruit sugar and 2
    tablespoons liquid honey
¼ teaspoon salt
1 tablespoon cream
125 g (4½ oz) plain chocolate

Method
Finely chop the mixed peel, cherries, sultanas, angelica, pineapple and apricots. Melt the butter in a saucepan over a low heat. Add the sugar and salt. Stir until the sugar dissolves and bring to the boil. Boil gently for a minute without stirring. Just as mixture is beginning to turn a light brown, add the cream, fruit and nuts. Stir well.

Spoon the heaped teaspoonfuls onto well-greased oven trays, allowing plenty of room for spreading. It is best to bake only four at a time. Bake in a moderate oven (160°C, 325°F, gas mark 3) for about 10 minutes or until golden brown. Remove from the oven. Push each florentine into a neater round shape with a spatula. Allow to cool on the tray for one minute, then carefully lift each florentine from the tray onto a wire cooling rack. Cool completely.

Melt the chocolate in a bowl in a saucepan of simmering water. Allow it to cool slightly. Turn the biscuits over so that the flat side is uppermost. Spread a teaspoonful of chocolate onto each to cover. When almost cool, make wavy marks with a fork in the chocolate. Refrigerate until the chocolate is set. Store in an airtight container.

Meringues

Fruit sugar will not make a crisp meringue, but all meringue recipes cook at such a low temperature that we can use ordinary sugar.

Ingredients
3 egg whites
150 g (6 oz) caster sugar
¼ teaspoon salt

Method
Prepare the baking tray by buttering and covering it with baking parchment. Beat the egg whites with salt until soft peaks form. Gradually beat in the sugar until completely dissolved. Place small spoonfuls of meringue on a baking tray, or pipe from piping bag fitted with a plain piping tube approximately 2 cm (½ inch) in diameter. Cook in a slow oven (130°C, 260°F, gas mark ½) for about an hour or until dry to the touch. Allow to cool with the oven door open. Remove from the parchment and stand on a cake rack. Store in an airtight container.

Almond and apricot meringue torte

Ingredients
4 egg whites
200 g (8 oz) caster sugar
¼ teaspoon salt
150 g (5 oz) chopped blanched almonds
80 g (just over 3 oz) dried apricots
1 tablespoon brandy
300 ml (½ pint) double cream
350 g (12 oz) can of apricots

Praline
100 g (4 oz) fruit sugar
2 tablespoons water
100 g (4 oz) chopped blanched almonds

Method
Place the almonds on an oven tray and bake in a moderate to slow oven for 5 minutes. Cool. Beat the egg whites with salt until soft peaks form. Add the sugar gradually, beating until completely dissolved. Fold in the first amount of almonds.

Butter two large oven trays, cover with baking parchment and butter again. Place half the meringue mixture on each tray in a matching round, about 25 cm (10 inches) diameter. Bake in a slow oven (130°C, 260°F, gas mark $\frac{1}{2}$) for about an hour or until dry to the touch. Change the position of the trays halfway through baking time. Remove from the oven, remove from the baking parchment and cool.

Cover dried apricots with boiling water and allow to stand for 20–30 minutes. Drain and purée in a blender or processor. Stir in the brandy. Whip the cream quite stiffly and fold into the apricots. Spread one third of the apricot cream over a meringue layer, top with the remaining layer, spread with the remaining cream, decorate with whole canned apricots and praline.

For the praline, place the fruit sugar and water in a small pan, stir without boiling until sugar has dissolved, boil rapidly until a light golden colour, add the almonds, pour the mixture onto a lightly greased oven tray and allow to set. Break into pieces and chop finely in food processor.

Petite coffee meringues

A change from after-dinner mints.

Ingredients
   1 egg white
   $\frac{1}{4}$ teaspoon salt
   $\frac{1}{2}$ teaspoon white vinegar
   75 g (3 oz) caster sugar
   1 teaspoon icing sugar
   2 tablespoons icing sugar extra
   2 teaspoons instant coffee powder

Coffee cream
   2 teaspoons instant coffee powder
   1 tablespoon hot water
   100 ml (4 fl oz) double cream

Method

Sift all the icing sugar. Grease two oven trays and cover with baking parchment and butter. Place the egg white, vinegar, salt and caster sugar in a small bowl and beat at high speed for about 10 minutes or until sugar is dissolved. Fold in 1 teaspoon of sifted icing sugar. Place teaspoonfuls on oven trays, trying to keep a uniform size, or pipe using a small plain piping tube. Bake in a slow oven (130°C, 260°F, gas mark ½) for about 40 minutes or until dry to the touch. Carefully remove from the baking parchment and cool.

For the coffee cream, dissolve the coffee powder in the hot water, cool and add to the cream. Beat until soft peaks form. Join meringues with the coffee cream, combine the remaining icing sugar and coffee powder and dust over the meringues on a serving plate.

Dawn's chocolate log

Because this cake contains no ground almonds, it is particularly delicate and may be difficult to remove, even from baking parchment. However, you should have no trouble if you butter the surface of a sponge roll tin or oven tray and cover with baking parchment, then butter the surface of the baking parchment.

Ingredients
3 eggs, separated
6 tablespoons caster sugar
75 g (3 oz) plain chocolate
1 tablespoon brewed coffee
about a tablespoon of sifted icing sugar
¼ teaspoon salt

Method

Melt the chocolate in a bowl over simmering water, add the coffee and cool. Beat the egg whites with salt until stiff. Beat the yolks with sugar until creamy. Add the chocolate and coffee mixture, beating to blend well. Gently fold in the stiffly beaten egg whites.

With a rubber spatula, spread the mixture onto the prepared pan in an oblong shape. Bake in a moderate oven (160°C–180°C,

325°F–350°F, gas mark 3–4) for about 15 minutes or until done. Remove from the oven and place a clean damp tea-towel over the cake. Turn upside-down onto the tea-towel, peel off the baking parchment and roll up along the length of the cake. Leave to cool. Unroll and fill with whipped cream. Reroll and dust with icing sugar.

Each serving contains more cream than cake, so the amount of ordinary sugar should not cause IBS problems.

Chocolate truffles

These have a hard, chewy consistency and a creamy taste because of the dried milk powder. They're full of calcium, so they're very good for you. As the recipe is not cooked, you can use either caster or fruit sugar.

Ingredients
60 g (2 oz) butter
4 tablespoons caster or fruit sugar
4 tablespoons mild-flavoured honey
4 tablespoons milk
175 g (6 oz) plain chocolate
17 tablespoons dried milk powder – either low-fat or regular
vanilla essence
1 cup chopped dates or sultanas
ground almonds

Method
Measure the dried milk into a mixing bowl. In a saucepan over a low heat, melt the butter, milk, chocolate, sugar and honey together, add the vanilla and pour into the dried milk mixture. Add the fruit and stir well to blend. This mixture thickens as it cools and may become quite stiff. When blended, either roll into small balls and roll in ground almonds, or place in waxed paper or foil, roll into a log and slice to serve. Set in the refrigerator.

Chocolate raisin bars

Ingredients
50 g (2 oz) raisins
2 teaspoons brandy
1 small (170 g) can Nestlé cream
75 g (3 oz) plain chocolate
100 g (4 oz) ground almonds
150 g (6 oz) milk chocolate or plain chocolate

Method
Sprinkle the brandy over the raisins and allow to stand for 2–3 hours. Place the first amount of plain chocolate in a bowl in a saucepan over simmering water and melt gently over a low heat. Add the cream and stir to blend. Remove from the heat, stir in the almonds and raisins and spread in an 18 cm × 18 cm (7 inch × 7 inch) buttered or non-stick baking tin. Chill. Melt the remaining chocolate over simmering water and pour over the chilled base. Chill to set and cut into bars. Store in the refrigerator.

Raisin clafouti

Ingredients
75 g (3 oz) raisins
125 ml (4½ fl oz) milk
350 ml (2½ fl oz) cottage cheese
3 eggs
80 g (3 oz) fruit sugar
¼ teaspoon salt
50 g (2 oz) ground almonds
50 g (2 oz) butter
grated zest of 1 lemon
1 tablespoon lemon juice
icing sugar

Method
Line a rectangular oven-proof dish or loaf tin with baking parchment. Sprinkle the raisins over the bottom of the dish. Place the remaining ingredients in a bowl and blend until smooth. Pour over the raisins. Bake in a moderate oven (190°C,

375°F, gas mark 5) 40–45 minutes or until the mixture is set and lightly browned. Remove and sprinkle with icing sugar. This can be served hot with cream as a pudding or cold as a cake.

Christmas cake

Ingredients
225 g (8 oz) butter
75 g (3 oz) fruit sugar or 125 g (4 oz) brown sugar
4 tablespoons liquid honey
¼ teaspoon salt
6 eggs
350 g (12 oz) finely ground almonds
500 g (1 lb) seeded raisins
juice of 1 orange
225 g (8 oz) currants
225 g (8 oz) sultanas
125 g (4 oz) mixed peel
125 g (4 oz) chopped glacé cherries
grated zest of orange
85 ml (3 fl oz) brandy or sherry
1 teaspoon almond essence
1 teaspoon vanilla essence
1 teaspoon bicarbonate of soda

Method
Prepare a 20 cm (8 inch) square cake tin by lining it with two layers of brown paper and then with baking parchment. Wash the orange well, grate the zest and squeeze the juice. Cream the butter, sugar, salt and honey, and add the eggs one at a time. Mix in the grated orange zest, fruit, orange juice, brandy and essences. Mix the bicarbonate of soda with the ground almonds and add. You can add 2–3 more tablespoons of ground almonds at this stage if you think the mixture is too sloppy.

Pour into a cake tin and bake for 3½–4 hours in a very slow oven (120°C–140°C, 250°F–275°F, gas mark ½–1) or until a skewer or large darning needle comes out clean when inserted in the centre. Allow the cake to cool in the tin for several minutes, then remove from the tin and put on a wire rack. The cake can be iced with marzipan icing (make sure it is completely starch-free).

Rich chocolate cheesecake

Ingredients
750 g (1½ lb) Mascarpone or Ricotta cheese
250 ml (8½ fl oz) sour cream
150 g (5 oz) fruit sugar or 50 g (2 oz) fruit sugar and 2 tablespoons
liquid honey
1 teaspoon vanilla essence
3 eggs
¼ teaspoon salt
200 g (8 oz) plain (dark) chocolate

Method
Prepare the tin or pan as instructed in the 'Superb Cheesecake' recipe (page 163). Melt the chocolate in a bowl over a saucepan of simmering water then remove from the heat.

Beat the cheese with an electric beater until fluffy. Add the chocolate, sour cream, sugar/honey, vanilla and salt. Beat in the eggs one by one. Pour into the prepared pan and bake in a moderate oven (160°C, 325°F, gas mark 3) for 1 hour. If the cake springs back leaving no fingerprint when touched in middle, it is ready. Turn off the oven and allow the cake to cool completely with the door opened. Refrigerate overnight. Serve with cream.

Easy Christmas pudding

This pudding can be steamed, but if you wish to boil it in the traditional way, have ready a square of unbleached calico 62 cm (25 inches). Before using, drop it into a large pan of boiling water and boil for 30 minutes. Remove the cloth from the water and wring it out well. (You'll need rubber gloves!) Spread the cloth out and cover liberally with ground almonds. The cloth can be left uncoated, but this will give a better 'skin' on the pudding. Also have ready several yards of string (not twine!) and a very large saucepan three quarters full of boiling water. There must be enough water for the pudding to float.

Ingredients
1 kg (2 lb) mixed fruit, chopped if necessary
3 eggs
75 g (3 oz) fruit sugar or 125 g (4 oz) brown sugar
4 tablespoons liquid honey
$\frac{1}{4}$ teaspoon salt
225 g (8 fl oz) double cream
85 ml (3 fl oz) brandy
350 g (12 oz) finely ground almonds
1 teaspoon bicarbonate of soda

Method
In a large basin, beat the eggs with the sugar, honey and salt until thick and creamy. Add the fruit, cream and brandy. Mix the bicarbonate of soda with the ground almonds and add to the fruit. Blend well. The consistency should not be too sloppy but this will vary depending on how finely the almonds have been ground. If you think it's necessary, add a few more tablespoons of ground almonds at this stage.

Turn out into the centre of the prepared cloth, gather the corners and sides around the pudding as evenly as possible, pull the corners tightly to give the pudding a good shape. Tie firmly with the string about 2.5 cm (an inch) or so from the top of the pudding mixture to allow room for expansion. Twist the string round the cloth about 10 times to give a good, firm seal. Make a handle from the string ends to lift the pudding out easily when cooked. Lower the pudding into water, put the saucepan lid on immediately and boil rapidly for 5 hours. Add more boiling water about every 20 minutes – the water must never go off the boil. When done, remove the pudding from pan and suspend it freely from the handle of cupboard door or between the legs of an upturned stool or hook – the pudding must be able to swing freely without touching anything. Leave overnight. On the day of serving, reboil for a further 1½ hours. Serve with brandy butter or starch-free brandy sauce.

Sauces and dressings

If you've only ever thought of sauces as being made with flour or cornflour, you're in for a pleasant surprise. Cream or wine sauces are delicious and very easy to make – cream *and* wine sauces are the ultimate. There really is never any need to thicken sauces with starch – they can all be made in other ways, whether we're talking about sweet or savoury sauces.

Standard crème fraîche sauce

This is a delicious substitute for any standard white sauce normally made with flour or cornflour. Many cooks wrongly think that crème fraîche will curdle if it is boiled – this is not so. The mixture will go through a curdling stage but if you continue boiling, it will reconstitute itself and become smooth.

Ingredients
> 250 ml (8 fl oz) crème fraîche
> salt and pepper
> juice of 1 lemon

Method
Place the crème fraîche over a gentle heat. Season to taste and simmer until thicker and smooth. Add the lemon juice and any of the following herbs or flavourings: chives, tarragon, chervil, marjoram or fish, poultry or meat juices. You can make it richer by adding a tablespoon of double cream.

Mock béchamel sauce
Omit the lemon juice, add 25 g (1 oz) butter and a pinch of dried onion granules and/or $\frac{1}{2}$ teaspoon of whole black peppercorns.

Mock mornay sauce
Make as for mock béchamel, but omit the onion granules and peppercorns. Remove from the heat and add half a cup (or so) of mild grated cheese (Emmental or Gruyère or other good melting cheese). Blend well and add two egg yolks one at a time, beating hard with a wooden spoon. Return to a low heat and bring barely to simmering point. Remove and season to taste.

Hollandaise sauce

Here is a modern version of this classic sauce, made in a blender or food processor. If you want to make it the traditional way, you'll find the recipe in most books. Not all contain lemon juice but I prefer the flavour – you can omit it if you wish.

Ingredients　　　　　　　**makes about 285 ml or 10 fl oz**
　2 egg yolks
　1½ tablespoons boiling water
　225 g (8 oz) butter
　1 tablespoon lemon juice
　salt to taste

Method
Gently melt the butter over a low heat without boiling. Skim the whey (white froth) off the top and pour the clear butter into a separate container discarding any watery whey at the bottom of the original saucepan. Put the egg yolks in a blender or food processor, begin to blend on a low speed, slowly adding the boiling water and then the clear butter very slowly in a thin stream. Blend for a few seconds, add the lemon juice and a dash of salt. Check the seasonings. Serve quickly or keep warm over simmering water for no longer than an hour.

Mousseline sauce
Fold in 2 tablespoons of whipped cream.

Anchovy sauce

Ingredients
　225 ml (8 fl oz) any starch-free mayonnaise
　1 clove garlic
　45 g (1½ oz) can anchovy fillets
　1 tablespoon starch-free tomato ketchup

Method
Drain and finely chop the anchovy fillets, crush the garlic and combine with the other ingredients.

Tartare sauce

Another modern easy-to-make version of a great classic.

Ingredients
100 ml (4 fl oz) any starch-free mayonnaise
1½ tablespoons sour cream
2 teaspoons fresh dill
1 teaspoon chopped chives
2 teaspoons chopped parsley
1 teaspoon capers rinsed in water to dilute brine
3 spring onions
1 teaspoon lemon juice
salt and pepper to taste

Method
Combine mayonnaise, sour cream and lemon juice. Finely chop all the herbs and blend well. Taste before you add any additional salt.

No-starch gravy

Method
Roast the joint or poultry by itself using a recipe from this book or your usual method. Roast any potatoes and parsnips in separate pan. To give the vegetables a better flavour, remove some of the pan drippings from the meat during roasting and pour over vegetables.

Remove the joint to a serving dish and keep warm. Tilt the pan to allow the fat to rise to the surface and skim the fat from pan drippings. Replace the pan on a low heat. If you have cooked, say, a turkey or a joint of meat in a long, slow cooking, especially if it contains fruit stuffing, you may not need to add anything to the pan drippings to improve the flavour other than a cup of water or wine.

Instead of a stock cube
If the pan drippings look pale and uninteresting you will want to add additional flavouring. Instead of a stock cube (which contains starch) you can now add any or all of these: a teaspoon honey-mustard or any sort of French mustard that takes your

fancy (as long as it contains no starch); a dash of lemon juice; 100 ml (4 fl oz) of red or white wine; a tablespoon of dried onions; a teaspoon of dried garlic; a pinch of herbs; a knob of butter. Stir all together over a slow heat, scraping the brownings from the bottom of the pan.

Instead of flour, gravy thickening or cornflour

Remove from the heat and add 1–2 tablespoons (depending on how brown you want the final mixture to be) of crème fraîche, Greek yoghurt or double cream. Stir all together. Replace on the heat and slowly bring to the boil and allow the gravy to simmer until you have the desired consistency, adjusting seasonings and adding more wine or water if you wish. The consistency of the gravy may not be as thick as a flour-thickened sauce, but it will be more delicious and will thicken on standing.

Bérnaise sauce

Ingredients
½ *teaspoon onion granules*
100 ml (4 fl oz) wine vinegar
1 level tablespoon chopped tarragon
2 tablespoons water
salt and freshly ground black pepper
2 egg yolks
100 g (4 oz) butter

Method
Bring the vinegar to the boil, add the onion granules and simmer until the vinegar has almost completely evaporated. Meanwhile, chop the butter into knobs and set aside. Add the tarragon to the pan and remove it from the heat. Add the water and egg yolks, whisking vigorously with a wire whisk or electric beater until the mixture is frothy. Return the pan to a low heat, whisk in the butter, knob by knob. The sauce should now be thick and velvety.

Rich pepper sauce for steak

Ingredients
50 g (2 oz) butter
1 tablespoon brandy
2 tablespoons red wine
1 tablespoon French mustard
1 tablespoon canned drained green peppercorns, crushed
225 ml (4 fl oz) cream – double or extra thick

Method
Cook the steaks in butter or oil or grill, as desired, remove and keep warm. Add the peppercorns and brandy to the pan drippings. Ignite the brandy, remove the pan from the heat and allow the flame to die down. Stir in the mustard, wine and cream, then bring to the boil, stirring constantly until the sauce slightly thickens. Serve over the steaks.

Hot mustard sauce for gammon

Ingredients
1 tablespoon Dijon mustard
2 tablespoons honey-mustard
1 tablespoon white wine vinegar
1 egg
2 tablespoons Greek yoghurt (or crème fraîche)
100–225 ml (4–8 fl oz) liquor gammon is boiled in

Method
Whisk the mustards, egg and vinegar together in a saucepan. Slowly add 100 ml (4 fl oz) of liquor and whisk until blended over a low heat. Add the yoghurt or crème fraîche and continue stirring well until the mixture thickens. Add more liquor if needed and remove from the heat. Pour into a warm sauce boat. This sauce will continue to thicken on standing. Thin by adding more liquor.

Bitter orange sauce for game or pâté

Ingredients
zest of 1 lemon
1 tablespoon lemon juice
1 cup orange marmalade – preferably a bitter type
2 tablespoons sweet sherry or port
1 teaspoon honey-mustard
4 tablespoons water

Method
Thinly peel the lemon with a potato peeler and cut the rind into thin strips about 5 cm (2 inches) long or use a zester. Bring the water to the boil in small saucepan and add the zest. Simmer for 5 minutes and remove from the heat. In another saucepan heat the marmalade over a slow heat until melted. Push through a sieve and discard the orange pieces. Return the marmalade to the pan, add the port or sherry and mustard. Squeeze the lemon juice and add to the marmalade with the water and lemon rind. Simmer gently over a low heat for a few minutes (leave the thin strips of zest in).

Garlic-cream sauce for fried chicken

Ingredients
$\frac{1}{2}$ teaspoon garlic granules
1 teaspoon honey-mustard or $\frac{1}{2}$ teaspoon honey and
  $\frac{1}{2}$ teaspoon Dijon mustard
1 tablespoon Greek yoghurt, crème fraîche or double cream
60–100 ml (2–4 fl oz) wine or water
salt

Method
Fry the chicken as desired and remove to a warm plate. Pour away the surplus pan drippings leaving a couple of teaspoons in the pan. Add the wine or water (or both) and scrape down the pan brownings. Add the garlic granules and mustard and blend. Add the yoghurt or cream, blend well and allow to simmer for a few minutes. Season to taste. If you need to dilute it, add more wine or water.

Wine sauce for grilled steak
Make in the same way but do not use water and omit the yoghurt or cream. Red wine is best.

Tarragon sauce for grilled meats

Ingredients
> 150 g (6 oz) butter
> 2 level tablespoons Dijon whole-seed mustard
> 1 level tablespoon chopped tarragon

Method
Melt the butter in a small saucepan but do not let it brown. Add the mustard and tarragon. Stir well to blend, allow to heat through and serve.

Cheese and wine sauce for fish

Ingredients
> 30 g (1 oz) butter
> 100 g (4 oz) mild grated cheese such as Emmental or Gruyère
> $\frac{1}{2}$ teaspoon garlic granules
> 1 tablespoon white wine
> 1 tablespoon double cream
> salt and pepper

Method
Melt the butter over a low heat in a saucepan, add the grated cheese, garlic and wine. Stir to blend well without browning on the bottom. Stir in the double cream, taste and add salt and pepper. The sauce can be thinned with more wine or milk. Serve hot over cooked fish or use as a cooking sauce when baking fish.

Sauce veronique

For grilled chicken or fish.

Ingredients
225 ml (8 fl oz) dry white wine
350 ml (12 fl oz) water
75 ml (2½ fl oz) dry vermouth
50 g (2 oz) butter
100 ml (4 fl oz) double cream
100 g (4 oz) white seedless grapes

Method
Combine the wine, water and vermouth in a medium-sized saucepan. Boil rapidly until it is reduced by half. Reduce the heat, add the butter and cream and stir until thickened. Add the grapes, reheat without boiling and serve.

Fresh tarragon sauce

For grilled meats, chicken or fish.

Ingredients
50 g (2 oz) butter
½ teaspoon garlic granules
2 tablespoons fresh tarragon
1 teaspoon mild Dijon mustard
1 teaspoon lemon juice
75 ml (2½ fl oz) brandy
100 ml (4 fl oz) cream

Method
Heat the butter, garlic, tarragon, mustard, lemon juice and brandy until boiling. Reduce heat and simmer uncovered for 2 minutes. Gradually stir in the cream, reheat without boiling, and serve.

Mint sauce

Ingredients
3–4 handfuls of fresh mint leaves
2 tablespoons granulated sugar
100 ml (4 fl oz) light malt vinegar
boiling water
salt to taste

Method
Place the mint leaves on a large chopping board and chop coarsely with a large, sharp knife. Sprinkle with the sugar and chop finely, holding the handle of the knife in one hand and the tip in the other. As the sugar and leaves become scattered, scrape them into a small pile and continue chopping, until the leaves are very fine and well incorporated into the sugar. Scrape into a small bowl or jug, barely cover with a little boiling water then add the vinegar and salt to taste. More sugar or vinegar can be added if desired.

Classic vinaigrette

Ingredients
1 tablespoon wine vinegar
$2\frac{1}{2}$–3 tablespoons best olive oil
1 clove garlic
salt and coarsely ground black pepper

Method
Peel the garlic, chop roughly on a chopping board, sprinkle with salt and crush with the blade of a knife, scraping up, sprinkling more salt and crushing again until a paste. Measure the vinegar and olive oil into a jar, add the garlic, add black pepper and shake until blended.

Make your own variations by adding any of these: a teaspoon Dijon mustard; a pinch of sugar; $\frac{1}{2}$ teaspoon of honey; whole green peppercorns and any non-starch seasonings such as steak seasoning, Italian garlic seasoning, etc. You should test them for starch before using. Aromatic vinegars, fruit vinegars, malt vinegars or lemon juice can also be substitued for wine vinegar.

Slimmer's salad dressings

Version 1 ingredients
$\frac{1}{2}$ *teaspoon garlic granules*
1 teaspoon Dijon mustard – any sort
150 ml (5 oz) mild unflavoured low-fat yoghurt
1 tablespoon lemon juice
$\frac{1}{2}$ *teaspoon non-starch tomato ketchup*

Method
Combine all the ingredients and blend well. Store in the refrigerator.

Version 2 ingredients
1 tablespoon low-fat yoghurt
1 tablespoon Greek full-fat yoghurt
1 teaspoon honey-mustard
salt and pepper to taste

Method
Combine all ingredients and blend well. Store in the refrigerator.

Caesar salad dressing

Ingredients
60 g (2 oz) grated Parmesan cheese
160 ml (6 fl oz) lemon juice
225 ml (8 fl oz) salad oil
100 ml (4 fl oz) olive oil
50–80 g (2–3 oz) can anchovies
1 teaspoon strong Dijon mustard
2 cloves fresh garlic, peeled
2 hard-boiled eggs

Method
Put all the ingredients in a food blender and blend well.

Honey lime dressing

Ingredients
   25 ml (8 fl oz) vegetable oil
   100 ml (4 fl oz) lime juice
   100 ml (4 fl oz) honey
   1 tablespoon grated lime zest
   $\frac{1}{2}$ teaspoon celery seed

Method
Wash the lime well, grate and squeeze the juice. Combine with the other ingredients.

Yellow brick bank dressing

A genuine recipe from the Wild West, named after an old bank.

Ingredients
   500 ml (18 fl oz) olive oil
   100 ml (4 fl oz) red wine vinegar
   1 egg
   2 cloves garlic, peeled and crushed
   2 teaspoons sweet Dijon mustard
   $\frac{1}{2}$ teaspoon dried oregano
   $\frac{1}{2}$ teaspoon dried dill
   salt and freshly ground black pepper to taste

Method
Combine all the ingredients in a blender. Store in the refrigerator.

Creamy blue cheese dressing

Ingredients
   70 g (about $2\frac{1}{2}$ oz) blue cheese
   100 ml (4 fl oz) double cream
   3 tablespoons lemon juice
   $\frac{1}{2}$ teaspoon fresh or dried chervil
   1 teaspoon fresh or dried tarragon
   pinch garlic granules
   salt and freshly ground black pepper to taste

Method
Mash the blue cheese in a bowl, add the double cream slowly and blend well – or blend in food processor. Add the remaining ingredients and blend again.

Green goddess salad dressing

Ingredients
  100 ml (4 fl oz) starch-free mayonnaise
  85 ml (3 fl oz) sour cream
  1 tablespoon tarragon vinegar
  1 tablespoon lemon juice
  ½ teaspoon dried onion granules
  2 anchovy fillets
  1 tablespoon chopped chives
  2 tablespoons chopped parsley
  1 clove garlic, crushed
  freshly ground black pepper

Method
Blend all the ingredients in an electric blender or food processor. Serve cold.

Old-fashioned orange sauce

Ingredients
  30 g (1 oz) fruit sugar
  1 tablespoon grated orange zest
  100 ml (4 fl oz) fresh orange juice
  50 g (2 oz) butter
  3 large eggs, lightly beaten
  1 tablespoon lemon juice
  pinch salt

Method
Combine all the ingredients in the top of a double boiler, or in a bowl inserted into a saucepan a quarter filled with water (do not let bowl touch bottom of saucepan). Stir well. Bring the water to the boil, reduce the heat so that the water is just simmering. Cook, stirring constantly, until the mixture is smooth and thickened. Serve warm or cold over ice cream or cheesecake.

Apricot sauces

Version 1 ingredients
  325 g can sugar-free apricots
  2–3 tablespoons fruit sugar
  30 g (1 oz) butter
  1 tablespoon apricot brandy (optional)

Method
Blend the apricots until smooth in a blender or push through a sieve. Place in saucepan with the fruit sugar and butter and bring to the boil. Simmer for a few minutes, remove from the heat and add the apricot brandy. Serve warm.

Version 2 ingredients
  175 g (6 oz) dried apricots
  500 ml (18 fl oz) water
  125 g (½ cup) fruit sugar
  1 tablespoon rum (optional)

Method
If the dried apricots are very hard, chop finely and soak overnight in the water. Add the sugar, then bring the chopped fruit to the boil, reduce heat, simmer for 15 minutes or so until the apricots are tender. Cool. Sieve or blend with the syrup in which they have been cooked until smooth. Add the rum.

Melba sauce

Ingredients
  1 pack frozen raspberries
  4 tablespoons fruit sugar
  1 jar good blackberry jelly (jam), such as Tiptrees

Method
Defrost the raspberries and purée in a food processor. Push through a fine sieve to remove the seeds. Place in a saucepan with the fruit sugar and bring to the boil. Simmer for a few minutes, remove from the heat and add the blackberry jelly, stirring until well blended. If the jelly does not melt into the hot raspberries, return to the heat for a few minutes, but try to combine them without extra cooking. Refrigerate and serve chilled.

Hot fudge sauces

Version 1 ingredients
250 g (1 cup) fruit sugar
175 g (6 oz) butter
125 g (4 oz) plain chocolate
2 tablespoons milk
dash salt

Method
Grate the chocolate into the sugar in a saucepan. Add the milk, stir well and place over a low heat. Add the butter, melt together and bring slowly to the boil. Taste and add salt. Boil for about 3 minutes, stirring constantly. Remove from the heat. This is a very rich sauce – less butter can be added if desired. Do not overcook as it will become too hard when cool.

Version 2 ingredients
75 g (3 oz) plain chocolate
225 ml (8 fl oz) sour cream
225 g (8 fl oz) fruit sugar or 100 g (4 oz) fruit sugar and 100 ml
    (4 fl oz) mild-flavoured honey
1 teaspoon vanilla essence

Method
Combine all the ingredients in the top of a double boiler or a bowl set into a saucepan of simmering water. Cook, stirring occassionally, for about an hour. This sauce will be thick and will keep for several weeks in the refrigerator. Makes about 500 ml (18 fl oz).

Caramel sauce

Ingredients
450 g (8 oz) fruit sugar
75 g (3 oz) butter
400 ml (14 fl oz) cream
dash salt

Method
Place the sugar, butter and half the cream in a saucepan. Bring to the boil over a low heat, stirring frequently. Boil for a few minutes then stir in the remaining cream. Taste and add salt. Boil for a minute or so extra, remove from the heat and serve warm.

Brandy sauce for Christmas pudding

Ingredients
  2 tablespoons fruit sugar
  100 ml (4 fl oz) water
  2 egg yolks
  pinch salt
  2 tablespoons brandy
  100 ml (4 fl oz) cream, whipped

Method
Place the sugar and water in a saucepan over a low heat and stir until the sugar dissolves. Bring to the boil, reduce the heat and simmer for 10 minutes. Beat the egg yolks and salt. Remove the hot sugar syrup from the heat and pour slowly into the eggs, beating until thick and creamy. Fold in the brandy and cream.

Sweets and candy

All these can be made with ordinary sugar or with fruit sugar. Fruit sugar is more expensive, but the advantages are considerable, as discussed earlier.

The most reliable way to test the cooking of sweets is with a candy thermometer. But I have had never had one. Instead, I learned the hard way – beginning at the age of about eight or nine, making toffee and fudge with my brothers and sisters, and never getting it right until we mastered the trick of the 'ball-in-the-water' test. It was a lot of fun, involving many tastes. We each had our own cup of cold water and usually consumed so much of the candy in various soft and hard ball stages that we were utterly sick of it when it was finally ready.

Here's how to test it. When the candy has been cooking for about the right amount of time as specified in the recipe, drop a little into a cup of cold water. Wait a few seconds and then test it between your fingers. If the right temperature has been reached, it will roll into a little ball, and depending on what you're making, this is how the balls should feel:

Fudge or caramel
A soft ball – not runny or sloppy but a definitely formed, soft ball which holds its shape.

Toffee and butterscotch
A hard ball – it should chink when you knock it against the side of the cup. This will produce a hard but chewy toffee. Some recipes say it should 'snap'. This means that the moment you pour it into the cold water it will immediately harden and become very brittle. This will be very hard toffee.

Toffee

Ingredients
    200 g (8 oz) fruit sugar
    100 ml (4 fl oz) water
    2 tablespoons vinegar
    $\frac{1}{4}$ teaspoon salt

Method
Place all the ingredients in a heavy saucepan over a medium heat. Stir until the sugar dissolves then boil, unstirring for 15 minutes or to a hard ball stage. Pour into a buttered dish and cool. Mark into squares before it is completely hard.

Chocolate fudge

Ingredients
> 100 ml (4 fl oz) milk (evaporated milk gives a lovely creamy flavour)
> 50 g (2 oz) plain chocolate, grated
> 500 g (1 lb) fruit sugar
> 125 g (4 oz) butter
> 1 teaspoon vanilla essence
> ¼ teaspoon salt

Method
Mix the sugar, salt and chocolate together in a saucepan. Add half the butter and slowly heat, stirring until the chocolate is blended in. Add the milk, stirring. Bring to the boil, stirring occasionally, then boil until the soft ball stage. Remove from the heat. Cool for 5 minutes. Add the rest of the butter and vanilla. Beat until thick, then pour into a buttered dish before it sets. Mark into squares and cut before completely hard.

Butterscotch

Ingredients
> 125 g (4 oz) butter
> 100 ml (4 fl oz) cold water
> 500 g (1 lb) fruit sugar
> 1 teaspoon cream of tartar
> pinch salt

Method
Put the butter, sugar, salt and water into a saucepan. Heat slowly and when the butter is melted, add the cream or tartar and boil for about 15 minutes or until the very hard ball stage. Pour into a buttered pan and allow to cool. Mark into squares and cut before completely hard.

Cream caramels

Ingredients
600 g (1½ lb) *fruit sugar*
125 g (4 oz) *butter*
450 ml (16 fl oz) *double cream*
½ *teaspoon salt*

Method
Bring the sugar, butter, salt and half of the cream to the boil, stirring constantly. Add the rest of the cream and continue boiling, stirring frequently until the hard ball stage. Pour into a buttered pan and cut into squares when cold.

Toffee apples

Ingredients
600 g (1½ lb) (3 cups) *fruit sugar*
1 *tablespoon vinegar*
1 *tablespoon butter*
4 *tablespoons cold water*
½ *teaspoon cream of tartar*
drop of red food colouring

Method
Have a number of apples ready on skewers. Boil all the ingredients together in a heavy-based saucepan without stirring until the very hard ball stage. Remove from the heat, dip the apples into the liquid toffee, then stand upside-down on baking parchment until hard.

Truffles

Ingredients
50 g (2 oz) *butter*
75 g (3 oz) *plain cooking chocolate*
150 g (6 oz) *icing sugar*
1 *tablespoon rum*
chocolate sprinkles

Method

Heat the butter and chocolate in a saucepan over a moderate heat until melted. Remove from the heat, add half the icing sugar and stir until thick. Add the rum and enough icing sugar to make a stiff mixture. Shape into small balls and roll in the chocolate sprinkles.

Relishes

I have not yet come across a commercially made chutney or relish that could be eaten on a non-starch diet. Most contain cornflour or other starch thickening. Fruit jelly or jam is a very good substitute to eat with cold meats or cheese. Red currant and cranberry jelly are traditional with game and ham, but if the general idea horrifies you, it is simply because you may not realise how similar 'jam' is to the chutneys and relishes with which you are familiar. They're both cooked in the same way with sugar – chutneys and relishes usually include vegetables, but not always; jams and jellies are sometimes made with vegetables, such as tomatoes and marrows. The main difference is that the chutneys and relishes have the distinctive flavour of vinegar and spices. You can achieve a very good substitute for this by combining jelly and mustard made with vinegar, such as Dijon mustard or honey-mustard.

Mustard fruits

Ingredients
1 pear
1 apple
1 orange
50 g (2 oz) green grapes
50 g (2 oz) black grapes
425 g (14½ oz) can black cherries
1½ tablespoons mixed peel
10 cloves
325 ml (12 fl oz) red wine vinegar
325 ml (12 fl oz) water
350 g (12 oz) fruit sugar
2 tablespoons hot Dijon mustard

Method
Sterilize two large preserving jars by immersing them in cold water with their lids and caps, bring to the boil and boil for 15 minutes. Leave the jars in the water until needed. Remove them one at a time.

Peel and core the pear and apple, cut into eighths then cut each slice in half. Wash and dry the grapes, drain the cherries.

Place the fruit in a large bowl, add the mixed peels and cloves and toss gently.

Meanwhile place the wine vinegar, water and sugar in a saucepan, stir over a medium heat until the sugar dissolves, bring to the boil, reduce the heat and boil gently for 5 minutes. Pack the fruit into the hot, sterilised jars. Add the mustard to the vinegar mixture, stir until combined. Stand the jars of fruit in a bowl or sink so that it doesn't matter if they overflow and pour the vinegar mixture over the fruit in the jars to cover completely. Keep for a week before opening and refrigerate when opened. Makes about 1 litre (2 pints).

Plum-orange chutney

This is quite tart, almost a sour mixture – a good substitute for piccalilli.

Ingredients
24 large plums
1 large orange
850 g (1¾ lb) seedless raisins
100 ml (4 fl oz) cold water
100 ml (4 fl oz) honey
2–3 tablespoons hot Dijon mustard

Method
Wash the plums well, pat them dry, remove the stones and cut into chunks. Wash the orange well and pat dry. Peel the zest thinly with a potato peeler, taking care not to include the bitter white pith, or use a zester. Remove all the pith and dice the pulp small. Cut the zest into very small pieces. Place the plums, orange pulp and zest, raisins, honey and water in a saucepan, bring to the boil and cook over a medium heat, stirring frequently until thick (about 45 minutes). Remove from the heat, stir in the mustard (taste and add more if you wish). Pour into sterilised jars as described in mustard fruits.

Plum sauce

Use instead of tomato sauce.

Ingredients
1.5 kg (3 lb) plums
750 ml (1½ pints) malt vinegar
400 g (14 oz) fruit sugar
2 teaspoons whole cloves
2 teaspoons whole black peppercorns
1–2 tablespoons honey-mustard

Method
Wash the plums well and remove the stones. Put all the ingredients except the honey-mustard into a large saucepan and boil together until reduced to a pulp (about 2½–3 hours). Remove from the heat, then stir in the honey-mustard to taste. Push through a sieve or blend until smooth. Pour into sterilised jars as described in mustard fruits.

Prunes in red wine

Ingredients
250 g (9 oz) pitted prunes
½ bottle red wine
sprig of thyme
sprig of rosemary
1 bayleaf
strip of lemon rind
1 tablespoon fruit sugar
1 teaspoon honey-mustard

Method
Combine the wine, herbs, lemon rind and sugar in a saucepan and boil until the liquid is reduced by about a half. Strain and return to the saucepan. Add the prunes and cook gently until plump and tender (10–15 minutes), remove from the heat and stir in the honey-mustard. Pour into sterilised jars with the liquid. Store in a cool place.

Orange curd

Ingredients
juice of 3 large oranges
3 eggs
75 g (3 oz) butter
225 g (8 oz) fruit sugar

Method
Whisk the eggs, sugar and juice together in a small bowl until blended. Place the bowl over a saucepan of simmering water (or in the top of a double boiler) add the butter and cook, stirring, until thick. Cook for a further 15 minutes. Pour into sterilised jars.

Flavoured butters

These are wonderful as toppings for grilled or fried steaks, chicken or fish. Combine the ingredients in a food processor, or with an electric mixer. Turn out onto wax paper or foil, roll into a log shape and freeze until needed. Slice onto hot food.

Herb butter
100 g (4 oz) lightly salted butter
2 tablespoons lemon juice
1 teaspoon chopped fresh thyme
2 teaspoons chopped fresh watercress
½ teaspoon chopped fresh rosemary
1 tablespoon chopped fresh parsley

Roquefort butter
100 g (4 oz) lightly salted butter
90 g (3½ oz) Roquefort cheese
1 teaspoon grated lemon zest
1 teaspoon hot Dijon mustard

Maitre d'hotel butter
100 g (4 oz) lightly salted butter
2 teaspoons lemon juice
2 tablespoons chopped parsley
1 tablespoon chopped fresh chives

Fruit stuffing for turkey

This gives enough stuffing for a small turkey of about 3.5 kg (6½ lb) – probably about half the size of most people's Christmas turkey. Increase the recipe for a larger bird.

Ingredients
  150 g (5 oz) stoned soft eating prunes
  250 g (9 oz) soft dried apricots
  300 g (about 3 medium-sized) eating apples
  3 tablespoons dried mixed herbs – any sort
  1 tablespoon garlic Italian seasoning (optional)
  ¼ teaspoon onion salt
  ¼ teaspoon onion granules
  1 teaspoon garlic granules
  sprinkle of salt and freshly ground black pepper
  2 eggs

Method
Chop the dried fruit finely and place in a large mixing bowl. Peel and grate the apples pouring away any excess juice and add to the dried fruit. Add all the seasonings and mix. Add the two eggs and mix again to blend all the ingredients. At this stage the stuffing may look too sloppy – don't worry as the eggs will bind it during the cooking.

Remove the turkey from its packaging and untruss. Remove giblets, etc., from neck- and leg-end cavities. Push stuffing into both ends of the bird, folding down the flap of skin at the neck end to hold the stuffing in, and pinning the leg end with cocktail sticks. Cook the turkey as desired.

Drinks

All these drinks contain fruit sugar (fructose) and are ideal to serve at a party, because as already explained in chapter 5, fructose increases the rate of alcohol metabolism and can help prevent hangovers. You can use fruit sugar as a replacement for ordinary sugar in your favourite punch or squash recipes.

Elderflower squash

Ingredients
   25 heads of flowers
   17 litres (3 pints) water
   1 kg (2 lbs) fruit sugar
   2 oz tartaric acid
   1 lemon
   4 oranges

Method
Place the flowers in a large bowl. Boil the water and pour over the flower heads and the sugar. Allow to cool, stirring occasionally. Wash the oranges and lemon well, cut up and add to the elderflower mixture with the tartaric acid. Leave for 48 hours, stirring occasionally. Strain and bottle.

Peach sangria

Ingredients   **Serves four**
   750 ml (1¼ pints) Chablis or other dry white wine
   4 tablespoons peach schnapps or brandy
   3 tablespoons fruit sugar
   1 fresh peach, peeled and thinly sliced
   1 orange, thinly sliced
   1 lemon, thinly sliced

Method
Combine the first three ingredients in a large jug, stirring until the sugar is dissolved. Add the fruit, cover and chill for at least an hour. Strain and pour into a serving jug. Serve over ice, adding fruit to each glass.

Amazing fruit squash

Ingredients
350 ml bottle or pack of orange or pineapple juice
150 g (6 oz) fruit sugar
1 teaspoon citric or tartaric acid

Method
Mix all the ingredients together and make up to 2.25 litres (4 pints) with water. More sugar or honey can be added to taste.

Strawberry champagne punch

Ingredients
3 punnets strawberries
100 g (4 oz) fruit sugar (more to taste)
85 ml (3 fl oz) Grand Marnier
2 tablespoons lemon juice
1.5 litres (2 bottles) champagne

Method
Wash and hull the strawberries and allow to dry. Save half a punnet and place the rest of the strawberries in a blender or processor, add the sugar, Grand Marnier and lemon juice, blend on high speed until puréed. Place the strawberry mixture in punch bowl. Just before serving add the cold champagne and remaining chopped strawberries. Makes about 2.5 litres (4½ pints)

Handy hints

Make your own stock 'cubes'

Save any pan drippings from roast meat or poultry. Pour into a container and allow to settle. Refrigerate. The meat juices will set into a jellied stock underneath the fat. When needed, skim the fat off the top and add the jellied juice to gravies, soups or any savoury dishes. The stock from chicken cooked with lemon juice and herbs makes an especially nice addition to salad dressings. If the fat is well skimmed off before cold, the meat juices can be poured into ice cube trays and frozen into cubes.

Herb cubes

Chop fresh herbs, either in single varieties or mixed, and pack into ice cube trays, adding a little water to hold in place. Freeze. Store the frozen cubes in freezer bags and use as required, simply adding to the dish during preparation.

Fresh herbs

Can also be frozen unblanched. Separate the leaves from the stalks and store in small freezer bags. Chop or crumble into food while still frozen.

Snacks

Silly snacks

Other people will think you're silly, but it tastes great! You need a packet of best-quality eating dates – the sort you buy for Christmas, some unbranded cream cheese (not Philadelphia) or some lightly salted butter (I prefer the butter). Slit each date open, remove the stone, place a sliver of cream cheese or butter inside date and eat. Great when you need something sweet. Similar to date scones – without the scone!

Savoury snacks

Thin slices of good Cheddar cheese wrapped in lettuce leaves make a quick and easy substitute for a sandwich.

Blue cheese is wonderful with sweet apples.

Cream cheese and chives are great with celery.

Try some thin processed cheese (or Dutch breakfast cheese) wrapped around a slice of ham or salami spread thinly with red currant jelly.

Try a slice of starch-free pâté on a slice of tomato.

Sophisticated snacks

Wash one or two small sweet apples, quarter them and remove the cores and cut into about eight slices. Cook in hot butter for about 3–4 minutes, turning once. Place on lettuce leaves on a plate and crumble some farmhouse Cheshire or crumbly Cheddar cheese over, add a squeeze of lemon juice and eat.

Sordid snacks

Pure greed and the secret knowledge that leftover baked apples may look awful but they taste great invented this snack. Scrape the cooked chilled flesh away from the skin, mash with a fork and fold into an equal amount of plain mild yoghurt or whipped cream.

APPENDIX: New research

Although you will not find information connecting IBS with starch intolerance in any other literature on IBS, or indeed, in any other medical books at the time this book goes to print, it has long been my belief that eventually doctors and nutritionists will begin to connect the pain and discomfort of IBS with the inability to digest starch. New information is now coming forward that points to a re-assessment of the effect of starch in the human digestion.

When I began to write this book in 1992, I had no information about the connection between starch and IBS, except the symptoms experienced in my own body. After I had contacted Dr Alan Stewart with my findings, he began to search for scientific information on the subject and discovered a number of papers that had been presented at a symposium on Starch in Human Nutrition in 1989.

It was too late to include these in the original book, but it was an enormous boost to my confidence to discover that I was not alone in pinpointing starch intolerance as a modern digestive problem.

New evidence

There is much new evidence emerging to show that the new processing of starches and the additional use of starch is certainly harmful to many people. Until the 1980s, it was believed that starch was an easily digested food which was totally absorbed by the human digestive system. However in the late 1980s nutritionists and scientists were beginning to have doubts.

In June 1989, the University of Saskatchewan, Saskatoon, Saskatchewan, hosted a symposium to discuss starch in human nutrition. Many new papers on starch were presented. In her introduction to the symposium, Alison M. Stephen of the Division of Nutrition and Dietetics, College of Pharmacy, University of Saskatchewan, says:

During the 1970s, considerable research had been devoted to dietary fibre and its role in prevention and treatment of disease. But by 1980, it was becoming clear that some of the effects attributed to fibre might in part be due to starch, which is present in many of the same foods. The decade of the 1980s therefore, saw an increased interest in the importance of dietary starch for human health and an exploration of the mechanisms by which starch might act at various levels of the gastrointestinal tract and elsewhere in the body. The fate of starch in the gastrointestinal tract emerged as a new area of study for the nutritionist and physiologist, as well as for the microbiologist investigating its fermentation in the large intestine ... Malabsorption of starch in the small intestine was discussed, including the emergence of the term 'resistant starch', that component which passes into the large intestine because of its resistance to hydrolysis and absorption in the small intestine. This was followed by papers on the fate of starch in the large intestine, the characteristics of its fermentation, and its effect on colonic function.

Starch and its behaviour in the human gut is now a major subject of scientific concern. Most research on starch digestion has been conducted on people with normal digestion. The papers presented at the Saskatchewan symposium were no exception, therefore the numbers of people suffering from an inability to digest starch, and the reasons for their inability, are unknown. But some reasons for a disabled digestion are known and have been known to medical science for many years. It is worthwhile considering these here:

Anti-biotics damage the gut

Doctors have long known that because antibiotics destroy healthy gut bacteria (as well as dangerous bacteria) they may promote gut disorders in both humans and animals. Drug companies producing these medications have long included such information in their data sheets and reference manuals. The damage has usually been considered to be temporary, but now it is thought that long-term damage to the digestion, may result from overuse of antibiotics.

In the introduction to his book, *Superbug,* Geoffrey Cannon says: *Most of 'Superbug' simply gathers together information published in textbooks and leading medical journals, and testimonies of leading research scientists, some specially interviewed for the book ... many research findings on ill-effects of antibiotics are new ... it seems to me that heavy or regular use of some antibiotics, liable to damage the mucosal lining of the gut wall and thus our immune defences, is for this and other reasons possibly one cause (please note, possibly one cause, not the cause) of a number of diseases that baffle modern medical science, some much more common in the last half-century. These include gut diseases such as irritable bowel syndrome, Chrohn's Disease and even colon cancer; some forms of arthritis; and the debilitating illness known as chronic fatigue syndrome or ME.*

Babies have trouble digesting starch

Before the age of four months, infants have only a limited capacity to digest starch. A baby's ability to digest starch increases slowly and even up to six months of age, is only partially developed – the reason why the recent addition of so much modified starch to processed baby food is a bad idea.

Starch is now added to almost every processed food

It is no coincidence that IBS is on the increase at a time when modified starch is increasingly added to our food. Look at the list of ingredients in almost any processed food in your supermarket. Most contain modified starch. This is increasingly true even of foods which would not include starch if you were making them at home – such as ice-cream and yoghurts.

- Modified starch is invariably added to low-fat foods. When fat is removed from foods such as ice-cream and yoghurt, the food will not thicken properly. Manufacturers therefore, usually add modified starch in some form, to give the required consistency. The words 'Low Fat' now almost guarantee the addition of modified starch.
- Prepared food ingredients now often contain modified starch. Pre-grated cheese, for example, is usually coated in modified food starch to keep the cheese from sticking

together. Often, sliced pre-cooked meat such as sliced turkey breast, contains modified starch.

- A new EC Directive now extends the range of permitted starches. Starches which were once not considered fit for human consumption in Britain, are now being added in highly modified forms to processed foods. These are especially permitted in foods for infants and young children classified as Weaning Foods, and for special medical purposes.

- The EC no longer requires starch to be identified in the ingredients list.

Starch is now no longer considered an 'additive' and is now permitted to be included in a food product in small amounts, without being identified in the list of ingredients. Already a number of European dairy products contain minimal amounts of starch, without saying so. I have discovered starch in yoghurts described as 'low fat natural yoghurts containing nothing but milk and bacteria'.

Starch in citrus fruits and apples

Citrus fruits

Further to my advice in Chapter 6 that most fruit contains fructose, I have discovered a number of fruits which also contain high amounts of starch in various parts, such as the skin. Oranges and lemons, for instance, contain a great deal of starch in the white pith. This is released when the fruit is squeezed or crushed, or when the skin is eaten. Obviously, less starch will be released if the fruit is very carefully peeled. It will depend on your intolerance levels, whether you are able to digest citrus fruits and juices, but if you find symptoms of IBS returning, I would advise elimination.

Apples

Sadly, I have discovered that some apples have very high levels of starch. These are sour or tart varieties, such as Granny Smith or Cox Orange. Sweet apples, such as Gala give a markedly different result when tested with iodine. I deduce that the starch in tart varieties does not all turn to fructose, and that this is enough to cause IBS symptoms when used either raw or in cooking.

Modern storage of fruit causes unexpected starch levels

Modern harvesting and storage methods are designed to delay ripening and prolong shelf-life. Most of the fruit we buy these days, has been kept in cold storage for some time in order to delay the ripening process. Usually it is picked before it is ripe. The irradiation process, used to prevent or slow down ripening of the fruit, is another factor which may prevent all the starch turning to fructose. If you have any doubts, just test with iodine.

So much to know – so little time!

Digestion is a long and complicated process not fully understood, even by experts. Food fashions come and go. Doctors and nutritionists change their minds about which foods are good for you, manufacturers pour enormous amounts of money into the promotion and advertising of various foods, and their public relations programmes influence even doctors and nutritionists.

No one yet knows why certain people cannot digest starch. Digestion varies from individual to individual and so it is very difficult to gain satisfactory results from people with 'normal' digestion – let alone on those with digestive problems. It may be that medical science will never produce a treatment or medication to overcome starch intolerance. A low-to-no-starch diet may be the only solution for most people.

BIBLIOGRAPHY

America's Best Recipes, Oxmoore House, Inc, 1993.

Australian Family Circle, *Cheesecakes, Puddings and Pies*, Advertiser Magazines Pty Ltd,

The Australian Women's Weekly, *Best Ever Recipes*, Australian Consolidated Press.

——, *Best Recipes from the Weekly*, Australian Consolidated Press.

——, *Best Ever Slimmers' Recipes*, Australian Consolidated Press.

——, *The Best Seafood Recipes*, Australian Consolidated Press.

——, *French Cooking Made Easy*, Australian Consolidated Press.

——, *Italian Cooking Class Cookbook*, Australian Consolidated Press.

'Bully Fare', The Volunteers of Theodore Roosevelt Inaugural National Historic Site, 1991.

Bailey, Adrian, *DK Pocket Encyclopedia, Cook's Ingredients*, Dorling Kindersley Ltd, 1991.

Barasi, Mary E. and Mottram, R.F., *Human Nutrition*, Edward Arnold, 1992.

Beeton, Mrs, *Book of Household Management*, Ward Lock and Co, 1906.

Belle Entertaining, Australian Consolidated Press, December/February 1990.

Better Homes and Gardens New Cook Book, USA, 1961.

Booth, Christopher C. and Neale, Graham, *Disorders of the Small Intestine*, Blackwell Scientific Publications, 1985.

Colden Country Cookbook, Colden United Methodist Women, New York, 1990.

Claire, Marie, *Cuisine Extraordinaire*, Conran Octopus, 1988.

Concise Family Medical Handbook, Collins, 1986.

Concise Medical Dictionary, Oxford University Press, 1987.

Crocker, Betty, *Betty Crocker's Picture Cook Book*, USA, 1959.

Currie, Donald J., *Abdominal Pain*, Hemisphere Publishing Corporation, 1979.

David, Elizabeth, *French Country Cooking*, Penguin Books, 1966.

Davies, Dr Stephen and Stewart, Dr Alan, *Nutritional Medicine*, Pan Books, 1987.

Davis, Adelle, *Let's Eat Right to Keep Fit*, Unwin Paperbacks, 1979.

——, *Let's Get Well*, Unwin Paperbacks, 1979.

Edmonds' Cookery Book, Edmonds Food Industries Ltd, 1986.

Farmer, Fannie Merritt, *The Fannie Farmer Cookbook*, Bantam Books, 1983.

Fox, Brian A. and Cameron, Allan G., *Food Science, Nutrition and Health*, Edward Arnold, 1992.

Galvani, Patrick, *Safeway Fresh Food Cookbook*, Octopus Books Ltd, 1984.

Grieve, Mrs M., *A Modern Herbal*, Penguin Books, 1984.

Goddard, Liza and Baldwin, Ann, *Not Naughty But Nice*, Ward Lock Ltd, 1987.

The Good Cook: Fish and Shellfish, Time Life Books, 1981.

Hanssen, Maurice, *E for Additives: The Complete E Number Guide*, Thorsons Publishers Ltd, 1987.

Johnson, Leonard R. (ed), *Gastrointestinal Physiology*, The C.V. Mosby Company, 1981.

McElroy, Mark and Sadler John, *GCSE Chemistry*, Longman Revise Guides, Longman, 1988.

McFarlane, Shona, *White Moas and Artichokes: Paintings, Prose and Preserves*, Hazard Press, 1993.

Neale, Graham, *Clinical Nutrition*, Heinemann Medical Student Reviews, Heinemann, London.

NZ Truth Cookery Book, Wellington.

1000 Cooks' Hints, Treasure Press, 1991.

Patten, Marguerite, *Cookery in Colour*, Hamlyn Publishing Group Ltd,

Parish, Peter, *Medicines: A Guide for Everybody*, Penguin Books, 1987.

Read, N.W. (ed), *Gastrointestinal Motility, Which Test?*, Wrightson Biomedical Publishing Ltd, 1989.

Roden, Claudia, *Mediterranean Cookery*, BBC Books, 1987.

Slater, Nigel, *Real Fast Food*, Penguin Books, 1992.

Slimming: The Complete Guide by the Experts of Slimming Magazine, Collins, 1993.

Souli, Sofia, *222 Recipes: The Greek Cookery Book*, Michalis Toumbis Publications SA, 1989.

Stewart, Maryon and Stewart, Dr Alan, *The Vitality Diet*, Optima, 1992.

Tarr, Yvonne Young, *The Ten Minute Gourmet Cookbook*, Lyle Stuart Inc, 1965.

365 Savoury Suggestions, Whitcombe & Tombs Ltd. Second edition revised.

Vogue Australia Entertaining Guide Winter '93, Bernard Leser Publications Pty Ltd, 1993.

——, *Wine and Food Cookbook*, Bernard Leser Publications Pty Ltd, 1989.

——, *Wine and Food Cookbook*, Bernard Leser Publications Pty Ltd.

Woman's Day, *Step by Step Cookbook*, Magazine Promotions Australia Pty Ltd, 1984.

Workman, Elizabeth, Alun Jones, Dr Virginia, Hunter, Dr John, *The Food Intolerance Diet Book*, Optima, 1986.

INDEX